AS in a wee[k]

Computing

Where to find the information you need

SUCCESS OR YOUR MONEY BACK

Letts' market leading series AS in a Week gives you everything you need for exam success. We're so confident that they're the best revision books you can buy that if you don't make the grade we will give you your money back!

HERE'S HOW IT WORKS

Register the Letts AS in a Week guide you buy by writing to us within 28 days of purchase with the following information:

- Name
- Address
- Postcode
- Subject of AS in a Week book bought

Please include your till receipt

To make a **claim**, compare your results to the grades below. If any of your grades qualify for a refund, make a claim by writing to us within 28 days of getting your results, enclosing a copy of your original exam slip. If you do not register, you won't be able to make a claim after you receive your results.

CLAIM IF...

You are an AS (Advanced Subsidiary) student and do not get grade E or above.

You are a Scottish Higher level student and do not get a grade C or above.

This offer is not open to Scottish students taking SCE Higher Grade, or Intermediate qualifications.

Registration and claim address:

Letts Success or Your Money Back Offer, Letts Educational, 414 Chiswick High Road, London W4 5TF

TERMS AND CONDITIONS

1. Applies to the Letts AS in a Week series only
2. Registration of purchases must be received by Letts Educational within 28 days of the purchase date
3. Registration must be accompanied by a valid till receipt
4. All money back claims must be received by Letts Educational within 28 days of receiving exam results
5. All claims must be accompanied by a letter stating the claim and a copy of the relevant exam results slip
6. Claims will be invalid if they do not match with the original registered subjects
7. Letts Educational reserves the right to seek confirmation of the level of entry of the claimant
8. Responsibility cannot be accepted for lost, delayed or damaged applications, or applications received outside of the stated registration/claim timescales
9. Proof of posting will not be accepted as proof of delivery
10. Offer only available to AS students studying within the UK
11. SUCCESS OR YOUR MONEY BACK is promoted by Letts Educational, 414 Chiswick High Road, London W4 5TF
12. Registration indicates a complete acceptance of these rules
13. Illegible entries will be disqualified
14. In all matters, the decision of Letts Educational will be final and no correspondence will be entered into

Letts Educational
Chiswick Centre
414 Chiswick High Road
London W4 5TF
Tel: 0845 602 1937
Fax: 020 8742 8767
e-mail: mail@lettsed.co.uk
website: www.letts-successzone.com

First published 2000
Reprinted 2001
New edition 2004, 2006

British Library Cataloguing in Publication Data
A CIP record for this book is available from the British Library.

ISBN 1 84315 582 6

Cover design by Purple, London

Prepared by *specialist* publishing services, Milton Keynes
Design and project management by Starfish DEPM, London.

Printed in the UK

Letts Educational Limited is a division of Granada Learning Limited, part of Granada plc.

An Introduction to Computers

15 mins
Time Yourself

How much do you know?

1 Give three examples of uses for communication and information systems.

2 Name three different applications of computer systems in the arts and media.

3 Internet banking can be viewed as being convenient because it means that customers do not have to travel to banks to carry out transactions. What is the other main advantage of Internet banking?

4 State the functions of embedded computer systems in three different domestic household appliances.

5 What type of computer system is likely to be used for weather predictions?

Answers

1 electronic mail, Internet, video conferencing, information kiosks, library systems, etc **2** animation, computer graphics, music, newspapers, etc **3** access to facilities and transactions 24 hours a day **4** temperature control – oven; timer control – microwave; program setting – washing machine/dishwasher, etc **5** expert system

If you got them all right, skip to page 6

Spend no more than 30 mins on this topic

DAY 1 2 3 4 5 6 7

An Introduction to Computers

Learn the key facts

1 Computers are widely used to communicate with other computers and people. The method of communication can vary depending on what the system is used for. Computers can be used to direct or transfer information, to send e-mails or for video conferencing. Computers connected to the Internet can access other computers' files and information. Many computers are used just to store large amounts of data and information (i.e. databases) for public or private access. Examples of such systems include public information kiosks, train timetables and fares and library systems. Other types of information systems include operation systems, management information systems, decision support systems and expert systems.

2 The use of computer systems is widespread in industry and commerce. These uses range from data processing (e.g. stock control, order processing), communication and information, to predictions for complex scenarios and situations (e.g. computers to predict nuclear reaction processes). Many computers influence the way we see and perceive the things around us. Television production is another sector dependent on computers, from small animations to large-scale computer graphics, and the control and order of programmes and advertisements. Computers now control the layout of most newspapers and magazines, and music and pictures are often digitised and manipulated.

3 As we attempt to make everyday tasks and activities easier and more efficient, computer systems play a more major role. From hospital waiting lists and traffic control systems to banking facilities and services, computers are making tasks much less demanding. Computing systems perform many operations like data processing and monitoring and control, reducing the demand for manual labour and intervention. This can often mean lower costs for manufacturing products and supplying services. Also, as computers do not need to eat or sleep, they can remain active around the clock. This allows many facilities and services to be accessible around the clock, e.g. cash machines, traffic signals and Internet banking.

4 Many of the monitoring and control systems found in industry, household appliances and cars are designed to perform specific functions and tasks. These systems are known as embedded computers (embedded microprocessor systems) and can control all the necessary functions of these devices. These systems can only perform a limited number of tasks but the devices they control usually only require a limited number of tasks, e.g. the control of temperature in a furnace or oven, or the control of cycles in a washing machine or dishwasher.

5 Systems that try to emulate human reasoning are called expert systems (or knowledge-based systems). Experts input rules and facts from a special field into the system, so that it can calculate and predict possible outcomes. These systems are used to give advice, as they are able to forecast and reason even with uncertain data. Expert systems comprise three basic parts, a knowledge base which contains all the known rules and facts about a subject, an inference engine which is the means of using the knowledge base, and a user interface which provides the user with a means of communicating with the system.

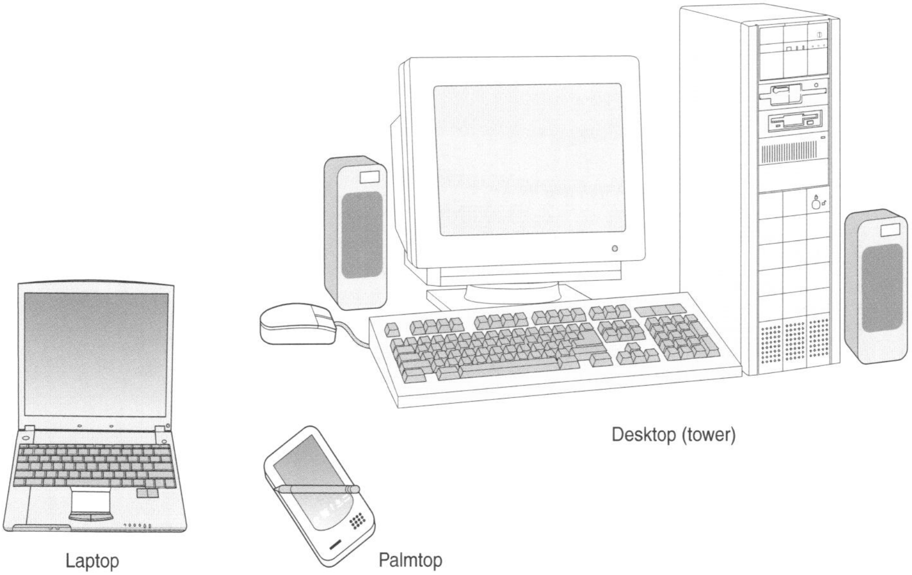

Desktop (tower)

Laptop

Palmtop

An Introduction to Computers

Have you improved?

1 Explain the general purpose of computers in:

a) stock control and order processing
b) traffic control.

think about the current manual system

2 What impact could Internet banking have on traditional high-street bank branches?

3 What possible disadvantages are there for the use of industrial robots in manufacturing?

4 Explain, giving examples, how embedded computers have made many household domestic appliances much easier to use.

how do your appliances work?

People and Computers

15 mins
Time Yourself

How much do you know?

1 State what effect the deployment of sophisticated industrial robots in factories has had on the unskilled workforce.

2 What is meant by the term data privacy?

3 Give four examples of computer crime.

4 There are two main categories of computer security measures. These are _______ security, which is the protection of actual hardware, and _______ security, which includes protection of sensitive information.

5 Outline the main objective of the Computer Misuse Act and the Data Protection Act.

6 Name two different occupations associated with the maintenance and use of computer systems.

Answers

1 reduction in unskilled workforce **2** data privacy is the term used to describe the need to keep sensitive data and information away from unauthorised persons **3** the deliberate destruction of data or information, the creation or distribution of viruses, the forging of documentation, computer fraud (for financial gain) e.g. theft of money or information **4** physical, software/system **5** to stop the misuse of data and information and computer systems **6** systems administrator, user support technician, technical support technician, etc

If you got them all right, skip to page 10

Spend no more than 30 mins on this topic

People and Computers

DAY 1 2 3 4 5 6 7

Learn the key facts

1 Computers and robots are now used to perform boring, monotonous and automated tasks in offices and factories. Computers and robots can improve the efficiency of many processes and reduce costs and can perform these tasks around the clock. Computers have brought about changes to methods of production and the development of new products and services. Hence, this has brought about changes in the working environment by removing the need for unskilled workers and increasing the need for skilled workers. More and more unskilled jobs are being lost whilst there is more demand for workers with information technology (IT) skills.

2 Data protection is becoming increasingly important. As well as ensuring that information and data is confidential and secure, it also important that the information and data stored is accurate. This is not solely for confidential data or information about individuals, but for all data. The prevention of data corruption and theft is essential, as these crimes can be very costly and disruptive to individuals and organisations. The correctness of data is termed as data integrity whilst restriction of data for authorised parties is called data privacy.

3 Computer crime is now taken very seriously, as the use of computers is now commonplace and, unfortunately, computer fraud for financial gain is becoming more and more widespread. Unscrupulous individuals and organisations have been known to use computers (and often specialist software) for the mishandling of monetary transactions. Other known forms of computer crime include hacking into computer systems to destroy or steal information, and the creation of viruses (which usually destroy or steal information).

4 Various measures have been implemented to combat the increase in computer crime. Measures taken for physical security include smart card, keys and video surveillance to reduce unauthorised access into buildings. This, along with the installation of other forms of security such as cables and clamps, reduces theft of physical items such as computer hardware. Software (system) security has also been improved by better management, and installation of specialist programs to protect data and information from security breaches via networks and modems. Other forms of software security include the encryption (putting into code) of data and the monitoring of computer usage.

5 Legislation was introduced in the form of the Data Protection Act and the Computer Misuse Act to try to curb the misuse of computers and data. The Data Protection Act (revamped in 1998) was introduced to prohibit the unauthorised storage of personal data as well as to regulate the authorised storage of personal data to ensure (as far as possible) that any data or information stored is correct and is used correctly. The Computer Misuse Act 1990 and other copyright legislation were introduced to stop hacking, copying copyrighted materials and the distribution of anti-social materials.

6 The widespread use and technical nature of the vast range of computer systems have created a variety of different occupations necessary for the use and maintenance of computers. These occupations range from user support, primarily helping users with the basic use and functionality of systems, to technical support, helping to identify and solve technical difficulties encountered when using such systems. There are also systems administrators, who configure the hardware and software on machines for use by others. This work often involves the setup of security measures and authorisation. Often, problems arise that are tackled by groups or teams of people. This calls for team-working with individuals having specific roles and different responsibilities for various parts of the task.

30 mins

Time Yourself

People and Computers

Have you improved?

DAY 1 2 3 4 5 6 7

1 Other than the initial purchase price of hardware and software, list four other costs associated with the installation and use of computers in the workplace.

2 Why is it important for organisations to keep a backup of data and information held on their computer systems?

anything can happen!

3 Explain why is it important to try to prevent the unauthorised copying of copyrighted software?

4 Suggest an argument against the monitoring of computer usage over the Internet as a measure of combating computer crime.

'Big Brother'

5 Explain the different uses of sophisticated filters in:

a) search engines
b) parental control.

6 Suggest why it is important for end users of computerised systems in industry to have:

a) user support
b) technical support

for the hardware that they use.

similar principles to using a video recorder

Software

15 mins

Time Yourself

How much do you know?

1 Name the main categories of computer software.

2 What is the difference between general application software packages and specific application software packages? Give an example of each.

Answers

1 general (generic) application packages; specific (special) application packages; programming languages – compilers and interpreters; operating systems; utility programs **2** general application software packages tend to be packages that perform a variety of general tasks, e.g. word processor, spreadsheet, whilst specific application packages are designed to perform a specific specialised task e.g. payroll, morphing programs, simulation programs, industrial robot control, etc

If you got them all right, skip to page 14

Spend no more than 30 mins on this topic

Software

Learn the key facts

DAY 1 2 3 4 5 6 7

1 Any changeable program, routine or procedure which instructs a computer system to perform a task is called software. Whether the system is a mainframe computer, an individual workstation or a manufacturing robot, it has to be given a set of instructions before it can perform a task. There are general (generic) applications, specific (special) applications, programming languages and tools, utility programs and operating systems.

2 General application packages tend to be appropriate to many areas and often include software packages found on most desktop computers. An example of the diversity of general application packages is a word processor's ability to produce forms, book structures and e-mails as well as standard letters. Specific applications packages are produced to perform a specific task, e.g. monitoring and control of a power plant.

Specific (special) application software

These are programs produced to perform a special function. They can be designed to run on any system from industrial machines to desktop PCs. Examples include robotics and control systems, morphing techniques, computer simulation (of aircraft), etc.

General (generic) application software

Word processors

These are applications that can be used to write, edit and format text to produce letters and documents (e.g. Microsoft Word). They often contain basic art functions to produce simple diagrams, charts and tables.

Spreadsheets

These are applications that can produce tables and charts, and perform mathematical calculations (e.g. Microsoft Excel). Basic accounts can be produced with 'what if' functions to help decision making.

Software

Databases

These are applications for data storage, retrieval and management (e.g. Microsoft Access). These applications contain appropriate links between the data to help the search and retrieval of information. They can often be accessed by different applications, e.g. a word processor for mail merging.

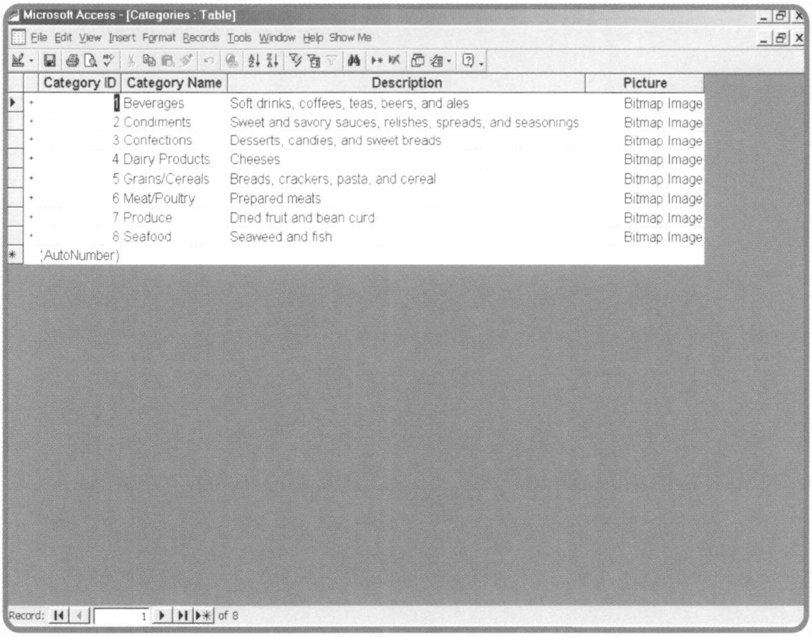

Desktop publishing

Applications for producing leaflets, newspapers, magazines etc. (e.g. Microsoft Publisher, QuarkXPress).

Presentation packages

Applications that can produce graphics, charts, tables, etc for making presentations (e.g. Microsoft PowerPoint).

Software

Have you improved?

1 A small company wishes to use a computer to produce its accounts, to store its customers' details and to send out monthly mail-shots to them.

a) What limitations would a spreadsheet have in keeping customers' details on file?

b) Suggest a more suitable application for this task.

c) What is an integrated package and why are they useful?

d) Give one reason why the company may not wish to purchase an integrated package.

e) Discuss the advantages and disadvantages of using a bespoke software package in place of a commercial (off-the-shelf) package.

what software do you have on your computer?

2 Give an example of a commercial product for each of the following:

a) word processor

b) spreadsheet

c) database.

Hardware

15 mins
Time Yourself

How much do you know?

1 What is usually the main difference between microcomputers and parallel processing computers?

2 In computing architecture, what is a bus?

3 a) What do the following acronyms stand for?

(i) RAM (ii) ROM (iii) CD-ROM

b) Which of the above can be termed as volatile and why?

4 a) Categorise each of the following peripherals into input and output devices.

(i) keyboard
(ii) monitor
(iii) printer
(iv) mouse
(v) scanner
(vi) digital camera

b) Give an example of how we may communicate with computers more effectively in the future.

c) Give two ways in which printed text can be input into a computer for editing.

Answers

1 parallel processing computers tend to have more than one processor and can thus perform two or more tasks at once (in parallel) **2** a means of carrying data from one component to another inside the computer **3** a) (i) Random Access Memory (ii) Read Only Memory (iii) Compact Disc Read Only Memory b) RAM is volatile as it loses all information when the power is switched off **4** a) keyboard, mouse, scanner, digital camera are input devices, monitor and printer are output devices b) voice commands or maybe even through thought processes c) keyboard, scanner (with OCR software)

If you got them all right, skip to page 18

Spend no more than 30 mins on this topic

Hardware

Learn the key facts

DAY 2

1 The majority of us are familiar with today's microcomputers. These are the types of computers found in most homes and offices (desktop PCs and laptops). They usually only have one processor, about 32 to 128 megabytes of memory, a hard drive, floppy drive, keyboard, monitor and printer etc. Mainframe computers are usually larger and can be found in companies that have many employees accessing the same system for different files. They usually have lots of memory and huge amounts of hard-disk space to keep numerous files and information.
A typical example would be a large database management system with millions of customers' details. Parallel processing computers have more than one processor so that several tasks can be done at the same time (in parallel) to reduce the overall processing time.

2 All computers share the same basic component structure. This consists of the processor (central processing unit), memory and input and output devices.

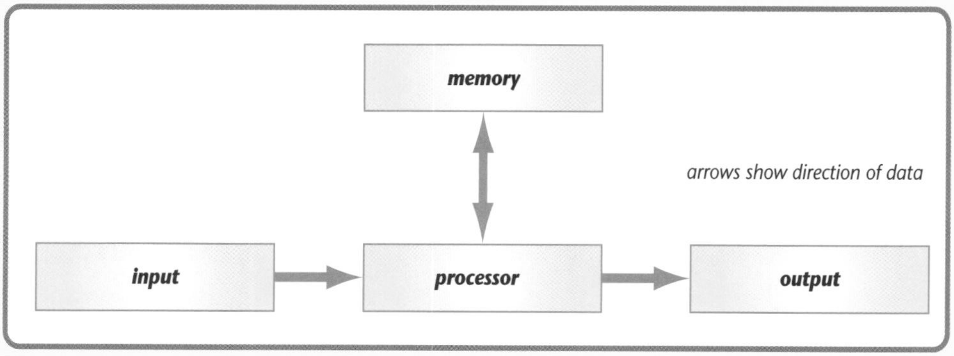

The processor (CPU) is central to a computer; data is input, processed and then output. The memory stores the instructions for the processor. The processor and memory communicate via buses; these buses carry signals and data between the two components.

The three standard buses are the data bus (two way) – needed to carry the data to and from the CPU and memory; the address bus (one way) – needed to carry the location of memory address; and the control bus (two way) – needed to carry the signal to tell the memory whether a read or write is in operation.

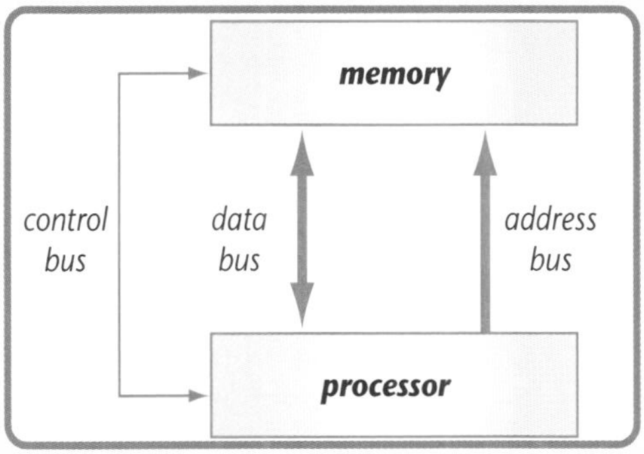

3 Storage on a computer can be split into two categories: primary storage (memory) and secondary storage (sometimes known as auxiliary storage). There are also two main types of memory, Random Access Memory (RAM) and Read Only Memory (ROM), both of which are primary storage. Random access memory means that any memory location can be accessed directly and the time taken does not depend on the location of the data. RAM is termed as volatile because it loses all information when the power is switched off. Compact Disk Read Only Memory (CD-ROM), Digital Versatile Disk (DVD), tapes and many other media disks are all forms of secondary storage. This is required to store larger amounts of data or programs on a non-volatile storage medium.

4 Peripherals are all devices that can be attached to the computer to perform specific tasks. Many peripherals are essential for computers to be of any use to us. The best-known peripherals are devices like monitors, printers, keyboards, mice, speakers, etc. All peripherals are input or output devices, or both input and output. An input device accepts data of one form or another and sends this as electrical pulses to the processor.

An output device decodes data from the processor and displays the information or stores the data for processing later. Less obvious input devices include touch screens, Optical Mark Readers (OMR), card readers, bar code readers, etc. Other output devices include speech output devices, sound cards and virtual reality helmets, etc.

There are many different hardware devices and media for various applications. The suitability of the device depends on the applications. For example, in systems like the national lottery where you are given a choice from a selection of possible numbers, or in a multiple choice examination sheet, mark sense or optical mark readers are used as an input device whilst a customised printer is used for the output.

30 mins

Time Yourself

Hardware

Have you improved?

1 Microcomputers are getting more and more powerful, with multiple processors, increasing amounts of memory and huge hard-disk storage spaces, yet the cost of these powerful microcomputers is falling. Explain what type of effect this could have on the distinction between microcomputers and mainframe computers.

imagine a world with only one type of computer

2 Describe (with the aid of a diagram) the functions of the three standard bus types in a computer.

what function do road buses perform?

3 CDs are increasingly being used in businesses to back up important files.

a) Suggest three advantages of using CDs to back up files in place of tape drives.

b) Give one possible reason why a company may not want to replace its existing tape-drive backup system with CDs.

why do some of us wait a little before buying the latest state-of the-art 66" TV?

Data Storage

15 mins
Time Yourself

How much do you know?

1 Explain the difference between data and information.

2 State a method of data capture suitable for (a) identifying a product at a supermarket checkout, (b) processing cheques, (c) inputting a player's choice of numbers in a lottery, (d) obtaining a customer's PIN at a bank's cash machine.

3 Consider this eight bit byte:

0	1	0	0	1	1	1	1

a) If this pattern represents a two's complement integer, state its equivalent in:

i) decimal
ii) hexadecimal
iii) BCD.

b) State what error condition would result if this number were multiplied by two.

c) If this pattern represents an ASCII value and the ASCII code for A is 65, give the character that would be represented by this number.

4 The method by which an image is represented in a computer file as a series of dots is called ____________.

5 State the data types suitable for storing the following items:

(a) a whole number (b) a number with a fractional part (c) true or false data
(d) a succession of keyboard characters (e) a person's name, address and telephone number.

Answers

1 data is basic facts, coded for computer processing; information is data with added structure or human meaning **2** a) bar code b) MICR c) OMR d) key pad **3** a) (i) 79 (ii) 4F (iii) 0111 1001 b) overflow c) O **4** bit map **5** a) integer or byte b) floating point or real c) Boolean d) string e) user defined/record

If you got them all right, skip to page 26

Spend no more than 30 mins on this topic

Data Storage

Learn the key facts

1 Data and information

Computers are data processing machines. As such, they operate on information that is coded in such a way that it can be handled by their electronics. Humans often require added meaning so that they can understand the data that they receive (information).

Computers store data as binary digits, so real-world information has to be prepared in some way so that the computer system can perform useful operations on it.

2 Data entry

Preparation of data for computer input can be done by humans or by various automatic methods. Generally, it is desirable to automate the process as far as possible to minimise human error and to maximise input speed.

Human data input
Keying in data via a computer keyboard or special keypad is often used to generate computer data in the first instance. Voice input may become more important in the future.

Automated data input
Swipe cards are useful for inputting a small amount of data such as a credit card account number. A small amount of data is stored on a magnetic strip.

Bar codes are used on retail items such as groceries and books. They are also popular for labelling stock items on warehouse shelves and for tracking the progress of items in warehouses and through delivery systems. Normally, a special scanner or a light-pen reads these codes. Bar codes store identity details such as product code or country of origin and never variable data such as price.

Smart cards are increasingly popular. They contain microchips, which can store much more data than magnetic strips. They are easily updated when used. They can be useful as cash cards, which can be topped up from time to time then used to pay for such small transactions as bus fares.

With Optical Mark Recognition (OMR), a pencil mark on a pre-printed form is read by an OMR reader. It is useful in, for example, recording students' marks in exams or any other situation where straightforward and simple data is recorded.

With Optical Character Recognition (OCR), a special font is used which is readable by both machines and humans. It is often used to record amounts in gas and electricity bills.

Magnetic Ink Character Recognition (MICR) is used mainly on cheques. This method is resistant to forgery attempts.

3 Data representation

Each memory location of a computer stores an eight bit pattern of zeros and ones. This pattern can represent an instruction or data. How it is interpreted depends upon where it is in the memory and how that part of memory is currently mapped.

Binary integers

Binary numbers are based on the concept of 'two'. There are two possible digits, 0 and 1. Each place in a binary number is twice the value of its neighbour to the right. Integers are whole numbers. Within a bit pattern, the value of a 1 depends upon where it is – in other words, its place value. The Most Significant Bit (MSB), is the leftmost bit, as it carries the highest value.

To convert a binary number to decimal, add together the place values of all the bits containing a 1.

	MSB							
place value	*128 (2^7)*	*64 (2^6)*	*32 (2^5)*	*16 (2^4)*	*8 (2^3)*	*4 (2^2)*	*2 (2^1)*	*1 (2^0)*
binary number	*0*	*0*	*0*	*0*	*1*	*1*	*0*	*1*

Thus we have one 8, one 4 and one 1.

8 + 4 + 1 = 13

In two's complement representation, the MSB represents a negative value.

When the MSB contains a 0, the number is positive.

MSB							
-128(-2^7)	64 (2^6)	32 (2^5)	16 (2^4)	8 (2^3)	4 (2^2)	2 (2^1)	1 (2^0)
0	0	1	0	1	0	0	0

The number above is:

$(1 \times 32) + (1 \times 8) = 40$

When there is a 1 in the negative MSB, the number must be negative.

MSB							
-128(-2^7)	64 (2^6)	32 (2^5)	16 (2^4)	8 (2^3)	4 (2^2)	2 (2^1)	1 (2^0)
1	1	0	0	0	0	0	0

The number above is:

$(1 \times -128) + (1 \times 64) = -64$

In any two's complement bit pattern the greatest possible number that can be represented will be a 0 followed by all 1s. The smallest (most negative) will be a 1, followed by all 0s. Thus, in an eight bit byte, the largest integer is 01111111, which equals 127 in decimal. The smallest is 10000000, which is –128.

Larger integers can be represented by using more bits. It is common to use two bytes (16 bits) to hold integers. In this case, the largest number that can be stored is:

0111111111111111 = 32767

and the smallest is:

1000000000000000 = –32768

When arithmetic is performed on binary numbers, the result has to be stored somewhere, in another memory location. If the result is too big for that location, the wrong result will occur.

For example, if we add 65 to 65,

0	1	0	0	0	0	0	1
0	1	0	0	0	0	0	1

we get

1	0	0	0	0	0	1	0

which is –126 and not the 130 we expect. This error is called overflow – the result is too big to fit in the required location. If the result is too small to fit in a location, the error is called underflow.

Hexadecimal

Hexadecimal (hex) numbers are base 16. These require 16 digits. There are no single decimal digits for the numbers 10–15, so we use letters instead:

0 1 2 3 4 5 6 7 8 9 A B C D E F

Each place value is 16 times the value of its neighbour on the right.

For hex value 21F:

place value	256 (16^2)	16 (16^1)	1 (16^0)
hex number	2	1	F

This is (2 × 256) + (1 × 16) + (15 × 1) = 543

Hexadecimal is useful as a shorthand for binary. Each hex digit is exactly equivalent to four binary digits, thus F (decimal 15) is equivalent to binary 1111. Most memory displays are given in hex to save space.

BCD (Binary-Coded Decimal)

In this system, each decimal digit is encoded as a separate binary number. To cover all the decimal digits (0–9), four bits are required per decimal digit. So, 461 in decimal becomes 0100 0110 0001:

0100 (4) 0110 (6) 0001 (1)

BCD is useful in calculators because each binary group equates directly to a decimal display digit.

Characters

The most common use of computers is to process text. This requires a means of storing characters. Characters are the symbols seen on a keyboard (letters, numbers and special signs) plus control characters which affect processing behaviour (e.g. ESCAPE, ENTER, LINE FEED).

Binary bit patterns can be interpreted as characters.

A table stores the equivalent character for any binary integer. Various systems have been used.

Note: the character 9 is not the same as the pure integer value 9.

EBCDIC (Extended Binary Coded Decimal Interchange Code)
This was once used by certain computer manufacturers, but is not in favour nowadays. The BCD system was extended to include characters as well as numbers. For example, 1100 0001 is equivalent to A. EBCDIC is an eight bit code allowing 256 different characters.

ASCII (American Standard Code for Information Interchange)
This is a seven bit code so it can store 128 different characters. This is sufficient for all the characters on a standard keyboard plus a number of control codes. For a long time it has dominated the world of data processing as there is much to be gained by having all computers using the same system.

Unicode
This has been developed to allow the encoding of languages that do not use Western characters, such as Japanese and Arabic. It is a sixteen bit code so it can cope with many characters. Currently, 24 language scripts are supported, including 34,168 characters.

4 Other data representations

Pictures and other images can be represented as a series of dots. The more dots per unit area, the better the quality. On a screen, images are made up of dots called pixels. Printed images are also made up from dots. A standard laser printer may produce up to 600 dots per inch in each direction. Dots can be represented in memory as binary bit patterns. Scanners can digitise images – that is, convert images into digital (binary) data.

Data Storage

A typical image may be made up from 1024 × 1024 dots. That is 1048576 dots in all. If each dot is represented by one byte, it can have any of 256 colours. This requires 1 Mb of storage. When each dot is separately stored or 'mapped', the method of storage is called a bitmapped image.

Sounds can be digitised. Sounds are wave forms and as such are analogue data. The sound can vary continuously in loudness (amplitude) and pitch (frequency). A sound wave is sampled at intervals, such as 22000 times per second, and a number is generated for each sample which corresponds to the height or amplitude of the wave. Such a system is used for CD recordings. This is an example of analogue to digital conversion.

5 Data types

When programming or otherwise setting up a computer system, it is necessary to define how the stored data is to be interpreted. Some common data types are given below:

Data type	Meaning	Typical Storage Requirement	Comments
integer	whole numbers	2 bytes, but 1 and 4 bytes are also common	Used in preference to floating point when speed of calculation is important.
floating point (real)	fractional numbers – also used for very large or very small numbers	usually at least 4 bytes.	Numbers are stored in two parts, the mantissa and the exponent. Possible to store a huge range of numbers. More complex to perform arithmetic than for integers so slower.
string	collection of characters	up to 256 bytes	These are commonly stored along with a length byte to indicate how much memory is occupied.
Boolean	yes/no data	1 bit (minimum) often 1 byte	Often used to perform tests in programs for decisions to be made.
user defined	often collections of other data types, grouped for ease of processing	as required	Useful for defining records incorporating a number of fields with different data types.

30 mins

Time Yourself

Data Storage

Have you improved?

1 Suggest ways of converting the following information into data suitable for computer processing:

a) the profile of a hill

b) a simple tune

c) the progress of a student.

2 a) A method of capturing data which requires someone to make marks on a form to represent numbers is called ___________.

A ___________ can store a great deal of data and is suitable for storing personal details on an identity card.

(b) Which of these data items might be stored in a bar code on a product in a supermarket?

(i) the size of the item

(ii) the identification number

(iii) the number of that item in stock

(iv) the price of the item

3 a) Convert the following two's complement binary numbers to decimal.

(i) 00011111 (ii) 11111111 (iii) 10000001 (iv) 11100011

b) Convert the following decimal numbers to hexadecimal.

(i) 31 (ii) 15 (iii) 255 (iv) 65

4 An image occupies part of a screen measuring 512 × 256 pixels. The screen can display 256 different colours. How much video memory is required to display the image?

how much storage is required for 256 colours?

5 A programmer defines a person's library record to contain the surname, forename, how many books are on loan and whether a fine is due. Describe the basic data types making up this record and explain how much storage one person's record would require.

15 letters is about right for each name

DAY 1 2 3 4 5 6 7

Data Structures

15 mins
Time Yourself

How much do you know?

1 You need to store the marks for ten assignments for each of twenty students. Describe a suitable data structure to allow this.

2 When a job is sent to a network printer, it is placed in a data structure called a __________. This ensures that all jobs are printed in the order in which they arrived. This data structure is known as a FIFO structure which means ______________.

3 If the words RED, BLUE, GREEN and YELLOW were input into a stack in that order, which of the following outputs would be possible?
a) BLUE, RED, GREEN, YELLOW
b) RED, BLUE, GREEN, YELLOW
c) YELLOW, RED, GREEN, BLUE
d) GREEN, YELLOW, RED, BLUE

4 Show how the following numbers would be stored in a binary tree for subsequent searching in numerical order:

4, 7, 8, 3, 1, 9, 5

5 A library stores details of books on a computer system. Users need to look up details of all the books by a certain author, one after another. Describe a suitable data structure to serve this purpose.

Answers

1 2-dimensional array of integers **2** queue, first in first out **3** a), b)

4

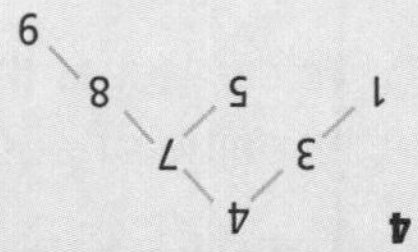

5 linked list. Each node stores article details with pointer to next article by same author. Index searched to find the first occurrence of author; linked list entered at that point

If you got them all right, skip to page 36

Spend no more than 30 mins on this topic

Data Structures

Learn the key facts

1
2
DAY
3
4
5
6
7

We have seen that there are basic primitive data types (such as string and integer) available in programming languages and software development tools. These can be used as building blocks to form larger data units, which allow efficient processing. These are called data structures.

1 Arrays

An array is a set of data items which are all of the same type. An array is fixed in size, so when it is set up (declared), the stated amount of memory is reserved, whether it is made use of or not. It is a static data structure as it will not change in size during use.

Arrays are made from elements. Each element is referenced by a number, its index. An array can contain data of any primitive type or combinations of such data. In other words, it is possible to set up an array of items such as integers, strings or records. Array elements occupy adjacent memory locations, which makes simple processing very rapid as an item can be directly accessed by its index.

A simple array of six integers is shown below. It is used to hold the results of a lottery draw, so its name is results. It could be declared in a program with a statement such as:

```
Dim results(6) As Integer
```

or something similar depending upon the programming language used.

index	*0*	*1*	*2*	*3*	*4*	*5*
value	*2*	*5*	*23*	*26*	*32*	*44*

Notice that we simply have one line of values: 2, 5, 23, 26, 32, 44. This array is therefore called a one-dimensional array.

We can get at the data in the array by referring to the array name and element, so the value of `results(2)` is 23.

Arrays can be made more complex if we need to hold data as a table. Suppose we want to hold the lottery results for four weeks. We can set up an array going in two directions. This is called a two-dimensional array.

We might declare this as:

```
Dim month_results (6, 4) As integer
```

The two-dimensional array called month_results could look like this:

index	0	1	2	3	4	5
0	2	5	23	26	32	44
1	3	16	23	24	33	39
2	6	22	35	37	44	48
3	1	26	35	40	45	49

Thus, for example, the value of month_results(4, 2)D.

2 Queues

Computing queues are like real-life queues. People (or items) join at the back and leave at the front. Queues are FIFO (First In First Out) structures. They are used for real-life applications such as keeping track of aircraft waiting to land at an airport, or for internal computer purposes such as maintaining a print queue so that print jobs sent to a network printer are processed in the correct order.

One way that a queue can be implemented is by means of an array plus two pointers. The pointers are integer variables that we shall call front of queue (FOQ) and back of queue (BOQ). In the case below, we have an empty queue. Both pointers point to the first element of the array. (FOQ = 0 and BOQ = 0). BOQ indicates where the next item in the queue will be placed. FOQ points to the next item to be removed. So when an item is placed into this queue, it is placed in the element pointed to by BOQ. Then BOQ is incremented.

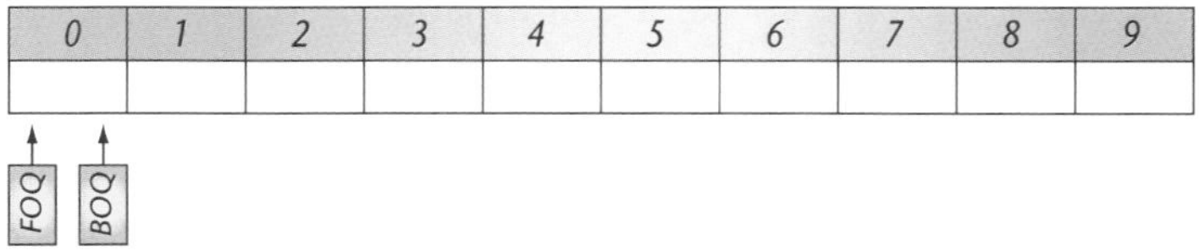

1
2
DAY
3
4
5
6
7

To place the name Anne in the queue, using an array called queue, the following actions occur:

queue(0) = "Anne"

BOQ is incremented, and so becomes 1, indicating where the next item will go.

The array now looks like this:

0	1	2	3	4	5	6	7	8	9
Anne									
↑ FOQ	↑ BOQ								

If more items are added, the queue might later look like this with BOQ set to 5:

0	1	2	3	4	5	6	7	8	9
Anne	*Karl*	*Joel*	*Amy*	*Charlie*					
↑ FOQ					↑ BOQ				

To remove an item from a queue, the data is not deleted, the FOQ pointer is incremented. To remove Anne from the queue, FOQ is incremented to 1 and we have:

0	1	2	3	4	5	6	7	8	9
Anne	*Karl*	*Joel*	*Amy*	*Charlie*					
	↑ FOQ				↑ BOQ				

This is a linear queue – the items form a line. There is a problem with this sort of linear queue: as items are added and removed, the queue moves through memory. Normally, therefore, once the end of the array is reached, the front elements are re-used. This is called a circular queue.

3 Stacks

A stack is structure that only allows items to be added and removed at one end. The first items get 'buried' under the later items. It is a LIFO (Last In First Out) structure. It is only possible to push an item onto a stack or pop an item from a stack. A stack, like any other data structure, is just a designated part of memory where these rules happen to be applied. It can, if necessary, be implemented with an array plus two integers – one to keep track of the current size of the stack and one to point to the top of the stack.

Stacks can be used to:

- check syntax during compilation
- store intermediate results during calculations
- store register values during subroutine execution
- store return addresses during subroutine execution
- reverse lists.

To reverse a list, consider a queue held in an array Q, containing the items ABCDE, with A being the front of the queue, Q(FOQ).

First, we remove items from the front of the queue and put them onto the stack. Push Q(FOQ) means push the item at the front of the queue onto the stack.

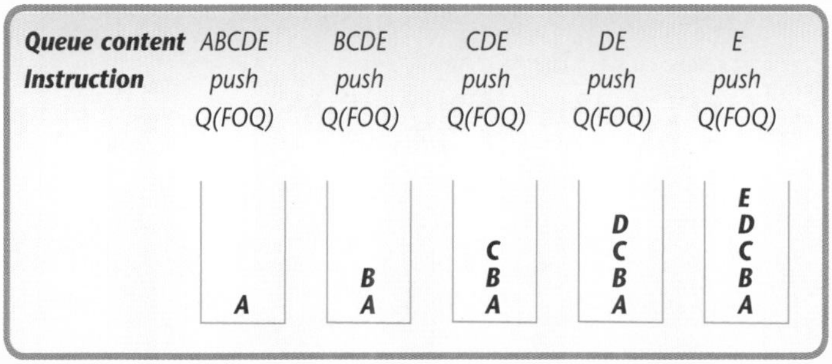

Then, we reconstruct the queue in reverse order by taking items from the stack and placing them one by one at the back of the queue. Remember, items join queues at the back and leave at the front. Pop Q(BOQ) means pop an item off the top of the stack to the back of the queue.

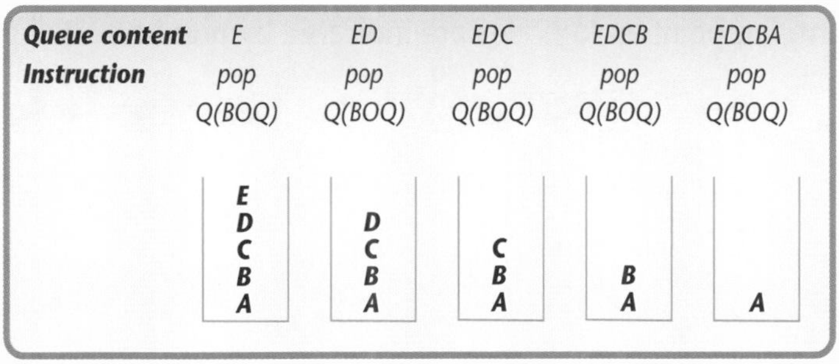

4 Trees

A tree is a structure in which each data item or node has pointers to other data items below it. It is a hierarchical structure. It is dynamic, which means it can grow or shrink as required. Binary trees have a maximum of two pointers per node. Trees originate from a root node. Nodes with no descendants are called terminal nodes.

Trees are common in computer systems. Most operating systems organise disk directories in a tree structure. Some databases are organised as trees to facilitate quick searching – the words in a spell-checker dictionary may be organised as a binary tree. Trees can be used to break down arithmetic operations into small steps.

Consider a list of words to go into a dictionary:

NODE, TERMINAL, BRANCH, HIERARCHY, DYNAMIC, ROOT, POINTER, TREE

To place the words into a binary tree, we follow these rules:

```
(take the items as they come)
place the first item in the root node
for each item
repeat
if the item is less (earlier in the alphabet) than the
current node, go left, otherwise go right until a null
pointer is reached
change null pointer to appropriate value
insert the item
set both pointers of new item to null
next item
```

In the diagram, the pointers to nodes are indicated by numbers. Null pointers are indicated by N.

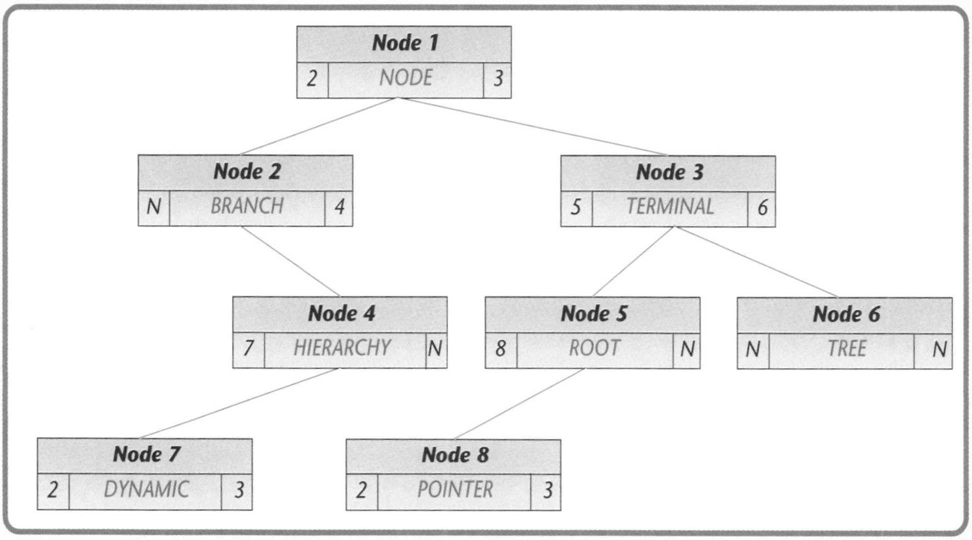

To search for an item in a binary tree, one method is:

```
start at the root
repeat
is the item the one required?
if yes then found
else
is the item less than the current node?
if yes go left
else
go right
endif
endif
until found or null pointer
```

5 Linked Lists

Linked lists are dynamic data structures – they grow and shrink as required. Each node contains data and a pointer to the address of the next node. An associated table stores the address of the start of the list (start pointer) and the next free space pointer, to show where to enter the next item in the list. It is efficient to alter the content or order of items in linked lists because very little movement of data is necessary – most alterations involve only changes to pointers.

The sentence 'Where do you want to go tomorrow?' is represented below. N represents a null pointer.

start pointer	*3*
next free space pointer	*8*

location	data	list pointer
1	want	2
2	to	5
3	Where	6
4	you	1
5	go	7
6	do	4
7	tomorrow?	N
8		
9		

Suppose we want to change this to 'Where do you *two* want to go tomorrow?' all we do is insert the extra word 'two' into the next free space (8), change the pointer for 'you' to 8, insert the pointer 1 to 'two' and finally change the next free space pointer to 9. This gives us:

start pointer	*3*
next free space pointer	*9*

location	data	list pointer
1	want	2
2	to	5
3	Where	6
4	you	8
5	go	7
6	do	4
7	tomorrow?	N
8	two	1
9		

Deletions are easily achieved by altering pointers. It is also very easy to recover data in order by following the pointers.

Several sequences can be stored simultaneously by storing more than one pointer per data item, so a linked list of records could retrieve references to a series of articles in order of author, subject or date.

Data Structures

Have you improved?

1 The months of the year are stored in a data structure so that they can be accessed by entering the month number.

Explain:

a) what data structure would be suitable for this purpose;
b) how the month of July would be accessed.

2 When aircraft approach an airport, if runways are free, they are told to land by the air traffic controller. If the runways are in use, the aircraft are made to circle overhead and await landing instructions. They are landed in order of arrival as soon as space is available. It is necessary to keep on the computer system details of such information as flight number, airline and airport of origin while they wait.

a) Describe a data structure suitable for holding this information and why it is suitable.
b) Explain how this structure could be implemented simply in memory.

3 a) Explain how a stack can be set up in memory, using an array and one integer variable.
b) What is the main shortcoming of this method?

4 A word processor's spell checker has a dictionary of 30 000 words. Describe a suitable data structure for the storage of the words and why it is suitable.

5 Describe how an item is deleted from a linked list.

Files

15 mins

Time Yourself

How much do you know?

1 Distinguish between files, fields and records.

2 A supermarket keeps details of all the products it sells in a database table. When stock runs low, the supermarket needs to generate an order to the appropriate supplier.

a) Suggest the contents of the entities (tables) required to implement these requirements.

b) Suggest key fields for this application and how they may be used to link the tables.

3 Explain the difference between validation and verification.

4 In what way do fixed-length records in a file make processing easier to implement?

5 Explain the difference between serial and sequential files.

Answers

1 files contain records, records contain fields **2** only some example fields given: a) stock_table: *product_code*, number_in_stock, reorder_level, supplier_code; supplier_table: *supplier_code*, supplier_name, supplier_address; order_table: *order_number*, supplier_code, product_code, number_ordered, date_ordered (b) key fields given above in italics. Link order_table.product code to stock_table.product_code; order_table.supplier_code to supplier_table.supplier_code; stock_table.supplier_code to **3** validation: software check that data is reasonable, at input time; verification: involves a human element, checking that data is accurate **4** processing involves records of known length so simpler search algorithms **5** both are stored one record after another, serial in no particular order, sequential in some order such as by key field

If you got them all right, skip to page 44

DAY 1 2 3 4 5 6 7

Spend no more than 30 mins on this topic

Files

Learn the key facts

1 File concepts

A file holds data. It is generally equivalent to a named quantity of data held on a storage medium such as a disk.

Text files are simply streams of bytes that represent characters. They can be displayed by simple operating system utilities and text editors. They are particularly useful when data has to be read on widely varying platforms, such as simple HTML pages on web sites. Programmers save source code as text files. Word processors add extra codes to text to modify the display of the text.

Binary files store streams of bytes that may be interpreted in various ways – for example, digitised images, sounds and program files that require the appropriate software in order to make useful information from them.

Structured data files hold data in a formal, regular way for data processing purposes. Such files are subdivided into components: the file structure.

A simple data file will contain data about a real-world entity. Such files can be regarded as a collection of records. Each record is a collection of fields. For example, for an entity such as a video collection, a file could contain hundreds of records. Each record is all the information on one video. A field is one item of data about an entity, such as the title of a video.

2 Databases

Databases are large assemblages of data, often stored as a single physical file on a storage medium. Such database files may contain a number of tables as well as other objects. Each table is chosen to hold data about one entity. These tables are the direct equivalent of the traditional files mentioned above – they contain fields and records.

By separating data into separate tables, most data can be held once only. For example, one and only one copy of a person's name will be stored. This helps ensure that there is no inconsistency caused by human error or updates.

The structure of a table in a database (or a simple data file) has to be determined before data can be entered. An example is shown below. In this case, the entity is a car in a used-car dealership.

Bear in mind that the data types and the field sizes may vary according to the facilities offered by the particular database system. For example, a field labelled as *Text* in one database system is equivalent to *String* in some programming environments. In the example below, *Numeric* is equivalent to *Integer*.

Field name	***Data type***	***Size (bytes)***	***Example***
Registration number	*Text*	*7*	*M264MRW*
Make	*Text*	*15*	*Peugeot*
Model	*Text*	*15*	*406 GLX*
Colour	*Text*	*20*	*China Blue*
No. owners	*Numeric*	*2*	*3*
Price	*Numeric*	*2*	*5000*

A file structure makes it possible to calculate how much storage is required for a database. A judgment is made on a suitable size for text fields. Database application development systems will often have their own default requirements for numeric and other data types. To work out the total requirements for a particular table, we can multiply the total byte count for one record by the maximum number of records expected, then add on an estimate for any overheads such as file header information. If we expected a maximum of 100 cars to be stored at any one time in this system, we would need the following storage space:

$(7 + 15 + 15 + 20 + 2 + 2) * 100 = 6100$ bytes

for the basic data plus a small amount extra to store header data such as the field names themselves.

It is usual to designate at least one field in each table as a primary key field. This is chosen to be unique so that a record can be unambiguously identified. Often, some sort of reference number is used for this purpose. In the above example, the car's registration number is suitable. Sometimes it is possible to combine two or more fields to make a compound key. In a table of hotel room bookings, a date plus room number will be unique.

Secondary keys can be useful in order to designate a number of records with something in common – e.g. the make of the car could be a secondary key.

Indexes are extra structures, which can be built into the database, and they store the position of records of a particular key value. Thus, an index of the make of car will allow a quick search to be made for all Ford cars, for example. Many indexes can be maintained for a database. Indexes can slow down database processing, as alterations to the data will have to be followed by rebuilding indexes.

Relational databases are collections of tables. In this context, a table is sometimes called a relation, a record can be called a tuple and a field an attribute. Joins are made between tables so that correct data from different entities can be accessed.

For example, in the car dealership, a table of car manufacturers may be required, so that the relevant company can be contacted for an enquiry regarding a particular car. A suitable manufacturer table could contain such fields as company_name, address, telephone_number. There would only be one entry for each manufacturer, so in this table, the company name could be a primary key. A join can be made between this field and the 'make' field in the car table, which *in this table* is known as the foreign key.

A foreign key does not have to be unique

This is a one-to-many relationship as shown in the crow's foot diagram below. This means that the dealership may have many Peugeots, but the Peugeot company details are only entered once.

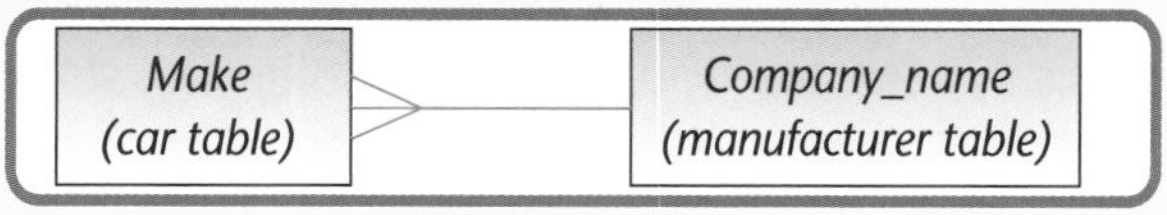

3 Validation and verification

It is of the greatest importance that the data held by an organisation is accurate. In some cases, the organisation's existence could be threatened by having bad data. Various methods have been developed in order to ensure, as far as possible, that data entered into computer systems is as reliable as possible. The methods fall into two categories.

Validation

This is a check performed on data as it is being input to ensure that it is reasonable. It is done by software to minimise human error. Some examples of such checks follow.

Type check: this ensures that data entered is the correct data type, such as that numbers are not entered for a field that requires letters only.

Length check: this prevents the entry of data that is too long for a pre-defined field.

Presence check: this ensures that a field is not left empty.

Range check: this makes sure that data falls within limits, such as that the date of birth is reasonable for a job applicant.

Picture check: this ensures that special formats such as post codes or car registrations are correctly entered.

Check digit: this applies an algorithm to the data entered and generates an extra character or digit. The same algorithm is applied when data is looked up, and if there is any error in input the check digit will be wrong and the operator alerted. Bar codes on most items have a check digit to ensure that scanning is successful.

Many applications avoid inaccurate input by arranging for data to be selected from pre-existing lists wherever possible.

Verification

This is a human check that data is *correct*. Source documents are scrutinised to see that they correspond to input data. One way to assist this process is to have two people type in data and the software compares the two versions. Any discrepancies are flagged so that the operator can check the source data.

4 Fixed and variable length records

When programming a database system, a choice can be made whether (1) to pre-determine the amount of space allowed for each record or (2) to allow it to accept whatever is entered. There are advantages and disadvantages to each approach.

Fixed-length

If fields such as *forename* and *surname* are defined as text and as having a maximum of 10 characters each, then all entries will occupy the 10 characters. So, when 'John Smith' is entered, the relevant characters are stored, plus spaces or garbage characters to make up the allocated space.

J	o	h	n							S	m	i	t	h					

This is obviously wasteful of storage space, but it does have the advantage that all records are the same size and it is easy to calculate the position of a particular record.

Variable-length

With this method, records vary in size according to need. To separate fields, a special character is used, often a comma or tab character. Such files are known as delimited or CSV (comma separated values). In the above example, 'John Smith' would be stored as:

J	o	h	n	,	S	m	i	t	h	,	

To access a particular record, each previous record would be visited and the end of field markers counted until the correct record was reached. Thus, storage is saved, but processing is slower and more involved. Another advantage of using delimited files is that most data processing software can read them.

5 File processing

Files can be organised in various ways. The method depends upon the processing needs and the nature of the storage device.

Serial files consist of records stored one after another. There is no particular order. They are commonly found in transaction files, where entities such as sales details are stored in the order in which they occur.

Sequential files are also stored one after another, but in a particular order, usually key field order. Master files (an organisation's main data files) are often stored in this way. Transaction files are often sorted into key field order before they can be used to update a master file. For example, a sales file may be sorted at the end of a day and each record used in order, to update stock figures in the stock master file. Serial files and sequential files can be stored on tape or disk. Data can be accessed by a sequential search – each record is examined in turn until the key required is found or the end of the file is reached.

Indexed sequential files are sequential files but an extra file – the index – is held, which stores the position of blocks of data. When searching for a particular record, the index is searched first to find the position of the block of data, then the main data file is accessed at the correct block.

Sequential files are commonly used when batch processing is carried out, i.e. when all the data to be processed is collected together and then the processing is run without the need for further intervention. Printing pay slips at the end of the month is one example.

Direct access files are used when it is necessary to locate a particular record straightaway without the need to read any previous records. These are useful when quick feedback is required, possibly with the need to update the record immediately. A typical example is when a travel agent checks the availability of a flight, then books it.

Records in direct access files must be stored on disk. There is usually some relationship between the key field of the record and the disk address where it is stored. In some cases, more than one record may be stored in a sector.

Hashing

Suppose 100 disk sectors are used for a file of bank accounts. Consider the account number 587453. The last two digits (53) could be taken to determine the sector where the record will go. So, all of the data regarding this account will be stored in that sector. This can be accessed directly from disk. However, account details for number 2564**53** will also go there. If there is room, it will be written after 587453 in that sector. So, if several records are written to the same sector, some degree of sequential searching will be required, but there is no need to search the entire file. This method (known as hashing) works best if the file is sparsely populated. Because customers come and go, not all the possible account numbers will be in use at any time. If a sector becomes full, any extra records that ought to go in that sector will be written into a special overflow sector.

30 mins

Time Yourself

Have you improved?

1 A college keeps data files about students. State the form of file storage that will be used to hold photographs of the students.

2 A table contains the following data about books in a book shop:

field	*data type*
ISBN (book number)	*text(13)*
author	*text(20)*
publisher code	*text(5)*
retail price	*floating point*
category	*text(2)*

a) Which field would be suitable as a key field?

b) If the shop held a maximum stock of 10 000 titles, calculate the amount of storage required for the data. Explain your assumptions.

3 An inventory of computer equipment is held by an organisation. Each record contains details of an item of equipment, including serial number, date purchased and category. Explain how length checks and range checks could assist in validating this data.

4 A very large database is to be sent to someone over the Internet. Comment on the advantage of using variable-length fields.

5 A hashing method is used to store stock records. Each record has a reference number. Each sector of storage is able to hold two records. The sectors are numbered 00 to 99. The hashing process determines where to store the record by taking the last two digits of the reference number.

The following records are to be stored in this order:

456, 876, 645, 856, 956

State the storage locations of the records.

Data Security and Integrity

15 mins

Time Yourself

How much do you know?

1 Distinguish between data security and data integrity.

2 List some methods of protecting data on a network from damage caused by unauthorised access.

3 Explain the difference between backing up and archiving.

4 The following bytes of data are transmitted from an on-line database. Even parity is used to ensure data integrity with the most significant bit being the parity bit.

a) 00110011
b) 01001010
c) 10010110
d) 01111011

One of the bytes contains an error. State which one and explain why.

Answers

1 security is the protection of data from unauthorised access or accident; integrity of data is ensuring that data is accurate and usable **2** identification, passwords, encryption, levels of access **3** backing up is making an extra copy of data for security purposes; archiving is making a historical record of data which is likely to be little used in the future; the original working copy is deleted **4** byte b). There are three data bits set to 1. Therefore the parity bit (MSB) should also be set to 1 to give an even number of 1s for the byte. Alternatively, one of the data bits is wrong

If you got them all right, skip to page 52

Spend no more than 30 mins on this topic

Data Security and Integrity

Learn the key facts

1 Keeping data safe

Data has to be kept secure. This means protecting it from loss or damage due to malicious actions or accident.

Malicious actions include:

- hacking, the illegal accessing of data, often via on-line links;
- damage from disgruntled employees who have access to a company's data;
- copying of data to gain a competitive advantage;
- alteration of data for purposes of malice or gain;
- data corruption by means of a virus or other malicious code. Viruses are programs designed to replicate and so spread to many files and computer systems.

Accidental damage can occur because of:

- fire, flood and similar hazards;
- equipment failure and power cuts;
- operator error.

Data integrity also needs to be ensured. This relates to the data being accurate. Accuracy depends upon:

- correct data input;
- correct data transmission;
- freedom from hazards which could corrupt data.

2 Protection from malicious acts

Most important corporate data is held on computer networks. This provides potential for unauthorised access from remote terminals. If a network is part of a Wide Area Network, or connected to the Internet, the number of access points is increased. Maintaining security is a matter of general strategy, in which a variety of methods can be employed.

Data Security and Integrity

Physical protection

Sensitive data can be confined to a single location, rather than placed on a network. Networked data can be made accessible only to certain workstations. There are obvious physical security issues, such as keeping rooms containing such workstations locked.

Software

- Screen savers that blank the screen and require a password for removal.
- Files and network access can be password protected. It is important that passwords are changed regularly and obvious words are avoided.
- At a network level, access to files can be fine-tuned so that only certain individuals or groups of individuals can access particular files.
- Files can be made read-only to prevent unauthorised changes.
- Data can be 'scrambled' according to a particular algorithm. Unless the receiver of the data has access to the decrypting algorithm, the data is unreadable.
- Software can be used to track the activity on a network. If unauthorised actions are discovered, details of dates, times, log-in identities, web sites visited and other information can be inspected.
- Firewalls are computers running security software that can be interposed between a network and the router to the Internet. They can be set to block certain sites and monitor all traffic.
- Virus scanning software can be installed, which checks disks and incoming files for malicious code.

General practice

- Codes of conduct can be put in place so that all employees regard security as an issue that concerns them.
- The use of disks brought in from outside can be banned to avoid virus risks.
- Downloads of files from Internet sites should be carefully controlled.

3 Safeguarding data

Valuable data should always be backed up. That is, a copy of up-to-date data is made on a backing storage medium and stored somewhere safe. If the worst happens and data is lost or corrupted, the only solution may be to restore it from a backed-up copy.

Strategies have to be decided upon so that a restore causes the minimal disruption to work.

In cases where the loss of *any* data could be critical, a simultaneous backup such as disk mirroring is sometimes used, whereby data is saved simultaneously to two disks. If one fails, the other can be used for a restore.

For individual use, where small quantities of data are involved, a backup to a floppy disk is a convenient method.

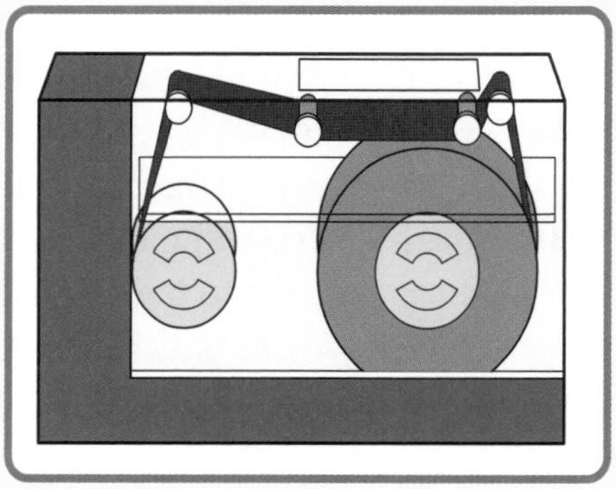

When large quantities of data are involved, such as on a network, a copy of critical data is saved to a tape as a batch process at pre-determined intervals. A tape is a cheap way of storing large quantities of data.

Frequency

The frequency of backing up depends upon how often the data changes. In most cases, a daily or weekly regime is considered suitable.

File generations

Where an organisation keeps a tape master file, such as for all its products in a stock control system, it will keep a record of sales on a transaction file. At intervals, the transaction file is sorted into key field order to make a sorted transaction file. This is merged with the master file to produce a sorted master file with the updated stock records. The old master file and the transaction file are kept until the next merge (or later). This enables the recreation of the updated master file in case of loss.

Network systems

A full backup (dump), is made from time to time so that a network's data and directory system can be recreated in case of disaster. This can be a long process and so, between full backups, it is common to make incremental backups. When a file is backed up, a file attribute (the archive flag) is set. If the file is updated, this is cleared. In this way, new or updated files can be identified for a partial backup. This data is appended to the backup tape and the process is quicker than for a full backup. Most organisations automate the backup process so that it takes place at night. This ensures that no files are in use, thereby getting missed in the backup.

Storage issues

It is important to keep backed up data safe in case it is needed. It makes sense to store it away from the computer system, so that in the case of a serious incident, such as a fire, the data will not be lost.

On-line storage is a convenient way to take this precaution. The backed up data is uploaded to a remote computer system.

In case of accidents to stored tapes, it is good practice to rotate the tapes used for full backups. If the last backup tape is lost or damaged, at least there is the possibility of restoring from a relatively recent one.

Archiving

Data is not needed in daily use forever. In a college, for example, the student data needed for day-to-day administration is not required after a student has left. Such data may be required later, say, for a reference, but this is not a regular occurrence. Old data which may be needed in the future is archived. This means it is copied onto a storage medium and the working copy is deleted, saving space on the live system. A cheap and convenient method of archiving is onto tape, but increasingly CD-ROMs are used.

4 Data in transmission

When data is being transmitted or input, various checks can be applied to ensure that the data has been copied correctly.

Batch totals

In a batch process, such as when a set of order forms is being input, the number of documents in the batch is recorded manually on a cover note. In this way, discrepancies can be detected at input time.

Data Security and Integrity

Control totals

To ensure that numerical fields such as order quantities and value are input correctly, the total of all the individual items in a batch is calculated manually and entered on the cover note. The computer then generates the same totals and generates a warning if there is a discrepancy.

Hash totals

This is a similar idea to control totals except that a meaningless total is generated for the batch, such as the sum of all the account numbers. Again, the computer verifies that the figure tallies with the total generated in advance. This has no processing purpose except as a check.

Parity checks

A common method of checking the integrity of transmitted data is the use of a parity bit. One bit of each byte sent is not used for data, but is reserved for checking purposes. In an even parity system, every byte transmitted is expected to have an even number of 1s. If the data bits have an odd number of 1s, the parity bit is set to make an even total. If the data bits already contain an even number of 1s, the parity bit is cleared. Thus, any received byte with an odd number of 1s must be in error. If two bits become corrupted, such a check may not work, so longitudinal parity checks are sometimes employed. In this, the bytes are grouped into blocks and an extra character, the Block Check Character (BCC) is added. This allows parity to be checked across bytes as well as within them.

	parity bit							
	1	1	1	0	0	1	1	1
	1	1	0	0	0	1	1	0
	0	1	1	0	0	1	1	0
	0	0	1	0	1	0	1	1
	0	0	1	0	0	1	1	1
	0	1	0	1	1	0	0	1
	1	0	0	0	0	1	1	1
	1	1	0	0	1	0	0	1
	0	1	0	0	0	1	1	1
BCC	0	0	0	1	1	0	1	1

The advantage of longitudinal parity checking is that double errors within a byte are more likely to be detected. Also, if an error is detected, there will be a parity error in the BCC as well as within the byte. Using the locations of these errors as co-ordinates, the faulty bit can be located and switched, thereby avoiding the need for a re-send.

Check sums

If the bytes in a block or data packet about to be sent are treated as integers and totalled, this total can be sent with the data. If the total is too large to be stored in the byte or word concerned, it is truncated. This is called a check sum. The total is recreated when the data is received and compared with the check sum.

30 mins
Time Yourself

Data Security and Integrity

Have you improved?

1 Explain the terms virus and hacking.

2 Suggest two methods by which data can be protected against virus attack.

3 a) Explain the meaning of the term incremental backup.
b) When is incremental backup preferable to a full backup? Why?

4 A company maintains a transaction file of products sold in the course of a day. Each sale generates one record. The data stored in the record includes: stock number, number sold, item price, sale total.

Explain how the following checks could be applied to this data:
a) control total
b) hash total.

Programming (1)

15 mins
Time Yourself

How much do you know?

1 Explain the differences between source code and object code.

2 A programmer needs to refer to the value of *pi* (3.142) throughout a program, and it is necessary to calculate the circumference of a circle on several occasions. Explain the declarations that would be needed to hold these values.

3 Given that = is an assignment operator, what would be the value of integer variable *i* after the following statements were executed in sequence?
(a) *i* = 4
(b) *i* = *i* * *i*
(c) *i* = *i* DIV 2

4 Explain the advantages of using procedures in programs.

5 Explain how a recursive procedure can cause a problem with the stack.

Answers

1 source code is plain text, written in a high level or assembly language. It cannot be executed directly by the processor. Object code is machine code, existing as bit patterns, which the processor can execute **2** *pi* would be declared as a constant as it would always hold the same value, whenever referenced. Circumference would be declared as a floating point variable, so that it can hold different values at different times and be able to store fractional numbers **3** a) 4 b) 16 c) 8 **4** easier debugging, tested procedures can be re-used, commonly used code can be called from various parts of the program **5** each time the procedure is called, the return address is pushed onto the stack. Recursive procedures are in danger of calling themselves forever, thereby filling the stack and causing a stack overflow error

If you got them all right, skip to page 62

Spend no more than 30 mins on this topic

Programming (1)

Learn the key facts

1 Types of programming

Programs consist of instructions. Instructions consist of two parts, an opcode (what to do) and usually one or more operands (what to do it *to*). For example, an instruction could be:

Opcode	Operand
copy into the DX register	*the number which is in the CX register*

Processors can only run instructions received as bit patterns. One pattern is interpreted as the opcode and another is the operand. The instruction above looks like this:

Opcode	Operand
10001011	*11010001*

The bit patterns of opcode and operand are stored in adjacent memory locations. The opcodes available to the programmer are laid down in the circuitry of the processor. The total of all the opcodes in a particular processor is its instruction set. A program consists of many of these instructions, carried out in turn. Instructions in bit pattern form are low level programs. Each instruction accomplishes just one operation – a one-to-one relationship.

Assembly language

Programming in bit patterns is not easy for human programmers – mistakes are easily made. Also, with only one operation per instruction, it is very laborious. Assembly language was invented to make it easier to remember the opcodes. Each one was assigned a small group of letters. This group is called a mnemonic because it reminds programmers of its meaning. For example, MOV means 'move'. The instruction above would look like this in assembly language:

Opcode	Operand
MOV DX	*CX*

This is still a one-to-one relationship, so it is still low level code. Processors don't understand words like MOV, so this has to be translated into the equivalent bit pattern by software called an assembler. Assemblers also allow parts of the code to be labelled and grouped into sections to make programming easier.

High level languages

Programming can be quicker if normal words are used instead of mnemonics. Many machine instructions can be grouped together to correspond to something the programmer wants to do. Rather than be concerned about moving bytes around, the programmer can concentrate on the bigger task. It is possible to put a message on screen by a simple command such as:

```
MsgBox("Welcome")
```

Statements like this are written in high level language. One high level statement results in many operations of the processor. This reduces program development time. High level languages are usually full of features that reduce effort. They have to be translated into machine code bit patterns before they can be run. Translation is done by either a compiler or an interpreter. The high level statements are written using a text editor and together, make up the source code of a program. When the code has been compiled, it is now in machine executable form, or object code.

Most high level languages are imperative, which means they produce programs that consist of a sequence of instructions – 'do this, then this, then this…'. There are some languages, such as LISP and Prolog, that work with a series of rules and relationships; these are called declarative languages.

Many programs nowadays adopt an interactive approach. They wait for the user to do something, e.g. click on a button, and then they respond accordingly. The user's action is called an event and the program is said to be event driven.

2 Elements of a high level language program

There are many high level languages, such as Visual BASIC, C++, Pascal, Delphi and Java. They all have their own characteristics, but they are all designed to make the work of the programmer problem-oriented, rather than machine-oriented. Certain concepts are common to most of them.

Programming (1)

Data types

Each programming language has a number of built-in data types provided with it. They vary between languages, but most provide a range of integers (of different sizes), reals or floating point numbers, booleans, string and character types. It is also possible for the programmer to construct new types by combining these built-in types.

Variables

Data handled by a program is stored in named sections of memory called variables. This data can be changed as the program progresses. It is easier to refer to names than to the memory addresses where the data is stored. Suppose a variable is set up to hold the result of a calculation. In Visual BASIC, we could write:

```
Dim result As Integer
```

This sets up two bytes of storage, somewhere in memory. (Most systems use two bytes for an integer). A table records that the variable result is to be found at that particular address. In fact, the address will not always be in the same place each time the program is run, but the programmer need not be concerned about that, the name is enough.

Variables should always be declared. This sets up memory space for them and also defines what data type they are. This allows checking later on that the right type of data is always assigned to them.

Constants

Any value that is required to be the same all the way through a program can be set up as a named constant. Reference can be made to the name without the need to enter its value at many places.

Variables and constants, and other named components of a program, are given their names by the programmer. The names are called identifiers. It is important that these identifiers mean something, so that as the program develops it remains easy to understand. This is especially important when there are many people working on a project.

Comments

All high level languages have the facility to insert comments in the program code. These are brief messages that help to remind the programmer what a particular line or section means when returning to it later. A special symbol is used to tell the compiler to ignore the comment line. Comments are not translated, so take up no space in the final compiled program. Comments are also useful in tracking down errors in a program. Lines can be 'commented out' in order to see if they are the cause of a problem.

3 High level language operators

Operators are the components of a program that make things happen. They can be placed in four main groups.

Assignment operators

These are used to assign a value on the right of a statement to a variable on the left. In most high level languages a statement will look something like:

```
Result = Number_1 * Number_2
```

The equals sign (=) is used in this example as an assignment operator. The statement means 'take the value stored in Number_1 and multiply it by the value stored in Number_2, then store the answer in the variable named Result'.

Arithmetic operators

These perform arithmetic on values. Most high level languages provide a set of suitable operators. Most require two operands, such as 4 * 2. Some examples are shown below.

Operator	**Meaning**
+	*add*
–	*subtract*
/	*floating point (real) divide*
DIV	*integer divide*
*	*multiply*
^	*raise to the power of*

Some arithmetic operators only work on one operand. They are called unary operators. For example, ++ in the C programming language,

```
Number ++
```

means increment (add 1 to) Number.

There is always an order of precedence for operators, such that in a complex expression, the operators are generally processed from left to right, but *, / and DIV are evaluated before + and −. Expressions in brackets are evaluated first.

Thus:

(4 + 5) * 3 = 27

but

4 + 5 * 3 = 19

String operators

One example of an operator working on a string is the concatenation operator. This is often the '&' character. Thus:

```
Full_name = "James" & " " & "Bond"
```

sticks together 'James', a space and 'Bond' to give Full_name the value 'James Bond'.

Boolean operators

These are used to compare values and produce a Boolean expression. A Boolean expression is one that evaluates to true or false. For example consider the Boolean expression:

```
Number_1 = Number_2
```

This is either true or false, depending upon what values are stored in the two variables. In this case, = is a Boolean operator (not an assignment operator, as seen earlier).

1 2 3 4 DAY 5 6 7

Some common Boolean operators are:

Operator	Meaning
= (== in C)	*equals*
>	*greater than*
<	*less than*
<=	*less than or equal to*
>=	*greater than or equal to*
! or <>	*not equal to*

4 Modular programming

Long programs are written in small sections or modules. The advantages of this approach are:

- Small sections are easier to debug.
- Once a module is thoroughly tested, it can be incorporated into the larger program with confidence.
- Modules can be re-used in different programs.
- Different programmers can work on different modules.
- Programmers can specialise in certain techniques.
- Modular code is easier to read, and hence to update.

Modules come in various guises. They used to be called sub-routines. The common module types nowadays are procedures, functions and objects.

Procedures

Procedures are self-contained pieces of program code, called from another part of the program. They carry out some action, but do not return a value. The following procedure is called *Multiply*.

```
Sub Multiply(Num_1 As Integer, Num_2 As Integer)
Dim Result As Integer
Result = Num_1 * Num_2
MsgBox (Result)
End Sub
```

Somewhere else in the program, the line

```
Call Multiply(4, 6)
```

calls the procedure and passes the values 4 and 6 to it. These values are called parameters. The use of parameters makes modules reusable for different values and saves programming size and effort.

When a procedure is called, it is necessary for the program to 'remember' where to come back to when finished. This is done by pushing the address of the next instruction onto the stack before the procedure is executed, then popping it off the stack when finished.

Functions

A function is similar to a procedure but it returns a value.

```
Function Multiply(Num_1 As Integer, Num_2 As Integer)
Dim Result As Integer
Result = Num_1 * Num_2
Multiply = Result
End Function
```

It can be called from within a line, e.g.

```
MsgBox (Multiply(2, 3))
```

Objects

These are modules that contain program code and data. They can be given properties and methods. Windows users are familiar with common objects such as menus, dialogue boxes, buttons and the like. They are useful because quite complex objects can be re-used in a flexible way without the need for extensive re-programming. A button is always a familiar button but it can have varying properties (size, position, the message on it) and varying methods (e.g. it can move to a different place or be made to respond to pressing the enter key).

5 Program flow

Selection

A program can be made to jump to a different point as the result of an event or a test. For example, if a program responding to temperature in a greenhouse receives an input lower than a critical value, it will jump to the code that activates the heater. Commonly, programming languages use structures such as if…then…else… to make such decisions. Selection can also be from a range of eventualities, sending program control to many possible points.

Iteration

This is the repetition of a section of code, sometimes called a loop. For example, a series of names might be put into an array and the input statements repeated as many times as is necessary. Iteration normally follows such constructs as:

Construct	***Meaning***
repeat…until	*Keep doing something until a certain condition applies. The condition is tested at the end of the repeated section.*
do…while	*As above, but test for the condition before executing the section.*
for…next	*Execute a fixed number of times.*

The syntax varies according to the programming language, but most languages support features of this sort.

Recursion

This is a special case of iteration, where a procedure calls itself. It has to be used with care, otherwise there is a danger that an infinite loop will occur. It is necessary to ensure that there is always a way out of the loop when a certain condition occurs, maybe after a maximum number of iterations. As procedure calls result in the return address being placed on the stack, if enough repetitions occur a stack overflow error will result.

30 mins

Time Yourself

Programming (1)

Have you improved?

1 Explain the difference between a low level and a high level language.

2 Explain what happens as a result of declaring a variable.

3 Evaluate

a) 5 + 8 / 2

b) (5 + 8) / 2

c) (15 + 4) – (3 + 2) * 3

d) 15 + 4 – 3 + 2 * 3

4 Show how a procedure and parameter passing could be used in a high level language to output the average of five numbers input by the user.

Programming (2)

15 mins
Time Yourself

How much do you know?

1 A programmer develops a module with the help of an interpreter. When it is completed, a compiler is used. Comment on the roles of these two translators.

2 Write a simple algorithm to check a series of numbers and output the largest.

3 Explain what is meant by top-down program design.

4 Distinguish between a translation error and a run-time error.

5 Explain how a dry run can be used to test an algorithm.

Answers

1 interpreter useful for interactive work – try one line at a time. Compiler needed to make executable program for distribution

2
```
largest_so_far = first_in_list
repeat
move to next position in list
read number
if number > largest_so_far
largest_so_far = number
until end of list
output largest_so_far
```

3 start with whole problem, successively break down into sub-tasks until modules written **4** translation error: syntax is wrong – rules of language contravened, detected by compiler. Run-time error: syntax is correct, but program logic is faulty, giving an incorrect result or other failure during execution **5** test data invented, value of variables written down after each program statement, see if they are as expected

If you got them all right, skip to page 69

Spend no more than 30 mins on this topic

Programming (2)

Learn the key facts

1 Program translation

A high level language program is written using a text editor. This may be part of a programming environment, but it still generates plain text. The code is called source code. It has to be translated to object code before the processor can run it. There are two approaches to this: interpretation and compilation.

Translator	Method of operation	Advantages	Disadvantages
Interpreter	Works on the stored source code directly. The interpreter translates the program line by line and executes it as it goes.	• Immediate feedback during development. • Can try a line at a time to see the result.	• Whole program slow to run as translation is required every time it is run. • User has to have interpreter. User has access to source code.
Compiler	Whole program translated, line by line, generating object code which can later be run.	• Code runs faster as no need for run-time translation. • User only has object code so cannot read/ interfere with source.	• When minor modifications are made, whole module has to be recompiled.

2 Algorithms

An algorithm is a description of how to carry out a process. It is useful to work this out in some detail before attempting to write program code. Traditionally, algorithms have been expressed as flow charts, but a series of statements is sometimes more convenient. When the statements approximate to program code, but do not necessarily follow the syntax of a particular language, they are called pseudocode.

Practice writing algorithms for a variety of simple problems.

Once the pseudocode has been worked out, the writing of real program code becomes easier.

Example: A common requirement is to find a record in a file. A sequential search is often used at some stage. What we basically want to do is establish what we are looking for, start at the beginning of the file, then check each record. If we find what we want, we look at it; if we get to the end of the file without finding it, it isn't there. This requirement can be turned into an algorithm as follows:

```
get key (what are we looking for?)
set file pointer to first record
repeat
read record key
if record key = key then found: output record: exit
move pointer to next record
until end of file
output "Key not found"
```

This could be written in slightly different ways, but it is getting close to legal program statements in a high level language.

3 Program design

The top-down approach

To solve a complex programming problem, it is sensible to split the problem progressively into smaller sub-problems, then continue splitting until manageable modules result. Many systems can be split up on a hierarchical basis as follows to produce a structure diagram.

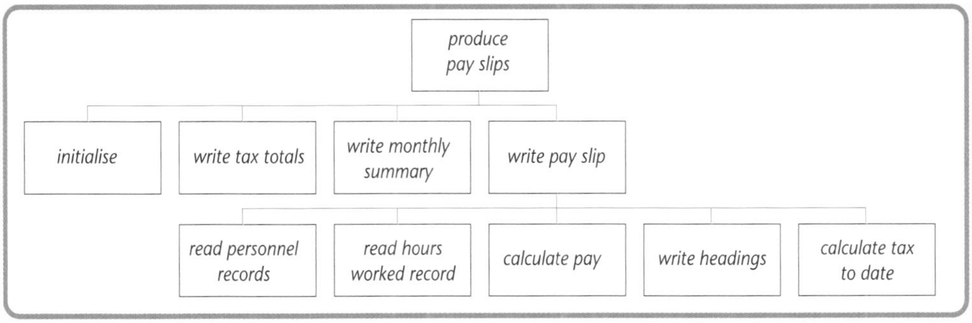

The lowest levels of such an approach can then be written out in pseudocode, which easily leads to the production of program code.

Formal methods are often used to impose a discipline on system development. This is useful where many programmers may be working on a project. Data flow diagrams are used at an early stage of a project's development. They make clear the overall movement of data through a system without concern for the precise details of coding.

The bottom-up approach

Sometimes it is useful to make the individual building blocks of a system and then stick them together later. Modern object-oriented techniques make this an attractive option as previously constructed and tested objects can be used with confidence in a larger system. With this approach, care has to be taken to keep the ultimate objective of the system in mind.

A combination of top-down and bottom-up approaches is often sensible.

4 Program errors

A variety of errors can occur during program development. Principally, they can be grouped according to where they have their effect. This will be either during translation, or during program execution.

Translation errors

If the programmer breaks the rules of the language, the translating software (compiler or interpreter) should detect this and produce a warning.

Syntax errors result from basic mechanical mistakes in coding such as mis-spelling a key word. Also included are faulty structures such as *if* without *endif* or unmatched brackets. Compilers will usually prevent such errors from being incorporated into the object code.

Semantic errors are where the meaning of the code is ambiguous or faulty. They may or may not be picked up by the translating software. Some languages allow the programmer to use variables 'on the fly' without declaring them. This could make possible the assignment of say, a floating point or character value to an integer variable. Some languages will execute such statements, possibly resulting in unexpected results.

Execution errors

These occur at run-time. They do not cause translation problems, but they can cause difficult-to-fix bugs at a later stage. For example, the well-known division by zero error can lead to program crashes. Also, problems can result from attempting to access a file that does not exist. Logic errors may not trigger any crash at all but a wrong formula can simply give the wrong results. Logic errors highlight the need for very careful and systematic testing procedures.

Programmers have the responsibility to incorporate routines to guard against user and logic errors. Mistakes made by users should be anticipated and not cause a crash. There should be error-handling routines which elegantly recover from mistakes.

5 Testing

With large and complex programs, it is difficult to remove all errors. Large and well known software companies are just as likely as anyone else to release faulty code. There are established methods of testing software, which take place at different stages of development.

Algorithm testing – dry runs

Some testing can usefully be carried out without a computer. A trace table is made and the column headings are variables, conditions or input/output. For example, consider the following code that is designed to count the words in a sentence:

```
Sub countwords()
Dim count, wordcount, length As Integer
Dim letter As String
Dim sentence As String
wordcount = 0
sentence = InputBox("Enter a sentence")
length = Len(sentence)
For count = 1 To length
letter = Mid$(sentence, count, 1)
If letter = " " Then wordcount = wordcount + 1
Next
MsgBox (wordcount + 1)
End Sub
```

Programming (2)

To check the performance of this piece of code, a trace table could be set up with headings for whichever variables you wanted to follow. A specimen sentence is written in under the 'sentence' heading and the code is worked through by hand. The boxes are filled in as you go, in order to check that the results are as expected.

count	*wordcount*	*sentence*	*length*	*output*

Debugging aids

Many programming language tools come with a debugger. These have various facilities to help the programmer check the code for logical errors. Commonly, they will have:

- a facility that lets you view the content of variables as the program progresses;
- a step-through option to execute a line at a time;
- a break point to allow the program to run to a given point then stop;
- a register viewer.

Testing strategies

When modules have been completed, they are tested to see if the output is correct for a given input. Data is input to cover all possible circumstances. Test data should include normal data, out-of-range data and erroneous data. No crashes should occur. Testing at this level, where the detail is not looked at but the outcome is examined, is called black box testing.

White box testing attempts to cover all the code in the program to reveal any logical errors. All pathways are considered.

Alpha and beta testing

Testing which is carried out in-house by the programmers' own colleagues is called alpha testing. Once the code is considered reliable, end users may be given an early copy of the software to try out in 'normal' conditions. They report back any further bugs that they find. This 'customer' testing is called beta testing.

Programming (2)

30 mins

Time Yourself

Have you improved?

1 A program written for a compiler runs faster than one written for an interpreter. Explain why this is so.

2 A procedure line writes a short line on the screen. The procedure *left* takes an angle as a parameter and moves the direction of writing that many degrees. Write a simple piece of pseudocode to input the number of sides and draw a polygon of that many sides.

3 Comment on the advantages of formal methods of program design.

4 Give an example of a programming error which could be detected by a compiler.

5 Describe the purpose of test data in a program module. How should test data be chosen?

15 mins

Time Yourself

Operating Systems

How much do you know?

1 What is:

a) an operating system

b) a network operating system?

2 a) Define the following terms.

i) file

ii) filename

iii) directory

b) Describe the main use of a directory.

3 List at least four different types of operational modes.

4 What is an interrupt?

Answers

1 a) a program that controls and manages the operation of the computer b) software enabling computers to communicate with each other over a network **2** a) (i) a collection of related records (ii) the name given to a collection of related records (iii) a group of files and/or subdirectories b) used to organise files into a manageable structure **3** batch processing, transaction processing, on-line, real-time, multi-access, process control, etc **4** a signal generated from a source or device requesting control of the processor from the current running program

If you got them all right, skip to page 74

Operating Systems

Spend no more than **30 mins** on this topic

Learn the key facts

1 An operating system is a program or set of programs that control and manage the complete operation of the computer. The operating system allows us to interface with the computer hardware. It can be described as the platform on which the applications that we use operate. Network operating systems allow computers to communicate with other computers over a network. Operating systems control resource management, input and output, interrupts, security and integrated utilities, etc.

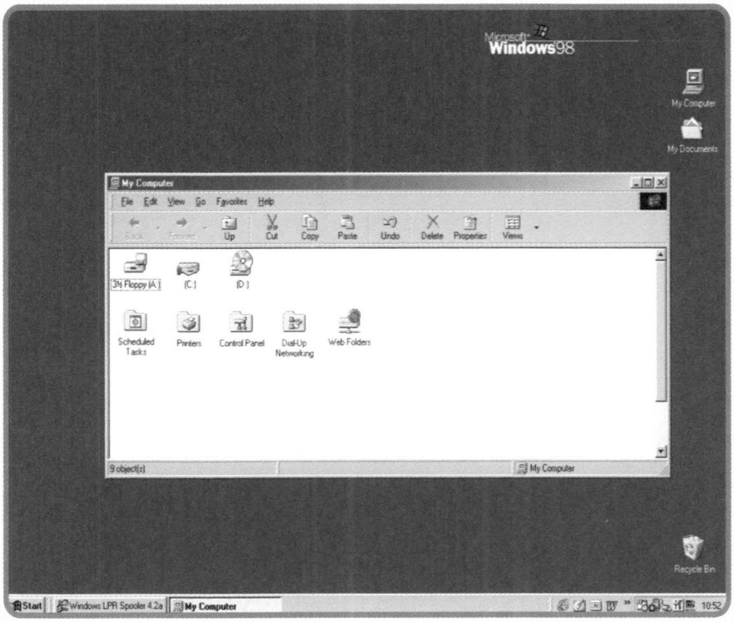

Resource management:

The allocation and scheduling of resources like processors, memory and input/output. The OS (operating system) controls which programs have priority over one another and how much of the computer resources are allocated to each task/program.

Input and output control:

Reading from and writing to the components and peripherals, e.g. processor, memory, backing-store, printers, VDU.

Interrupt handling:
Controlling breaks (deliberate or otherwise) in between activities to determine the next usage of processor time. Interrupts can be generated by current program, by a timer or by hardware devices.

Security:
Control of passwords and user access rights and privileges.

Utilities:
Control of programs for file and resource management, e.g. file transfer, reorganisation, editing, disk space, backup, etc.

2 A file is an organised collection of information or records. Each record is then made up of fields, and each field is made up of characters. Filenames distinguish one file from another. These files can be organised in a structure of directories (folders) and sub-directories with pathnames to locate where in the structure a file is stored.

Typical directory structure

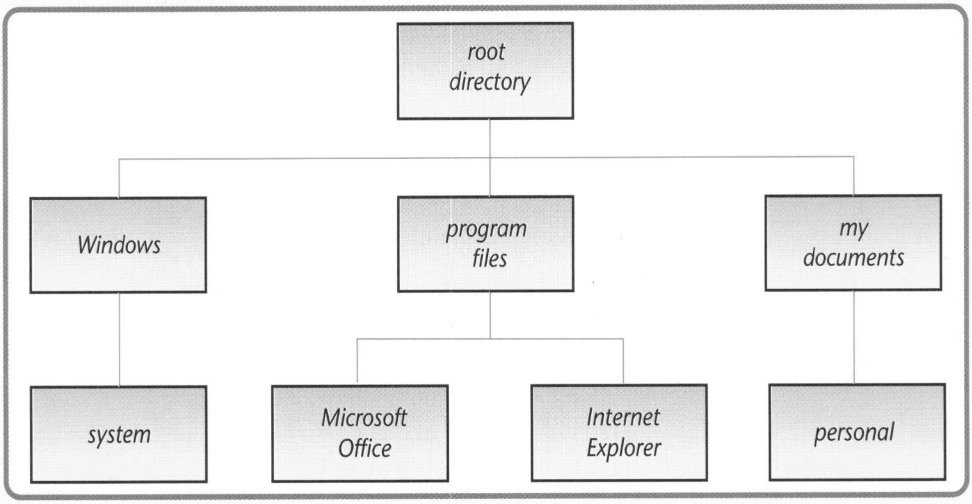

3 There are a variety of different types of operating modes for different applications.

Batch processing
These operating modes do not require the user to be present when performing tasks. Jobs or tasks can be submitted and queued until they are processed or all data is collected, before being processed together. Examples of batch processing operating systems are those of banks that regularly produce customer statements.

Real time processing

These operating systems process data at speeds sufficient to respond to requests and influence external behaviour. Real time processing systems can also be interactive, like those of cash machines that respond to our instructions for balances or cash withdrawals. The systems do not necessarily need to be extremely fast, but sufficient to process and respond to our requests. These systems are usually on-line, i.e. connected directly to a computer.

Multi-access

These systems allow more than one user access to a computer. This is usually done by using multi-processor systems or by time-sharing, i.e. allocating a specific amount of processor time between users.

Transaction

These systems deal with one transaction at a time. Each transaction must be completed before the next one begins.

4 When a device or program sends a signal to the processor interrupting the current running process, this signal is called an interrupt. The signal is sent because the device or program sending it requires the control of the processor. The current running program is suspended and the control of the processor is passed over to the new device or program. The old program is resumed when the new system no longer requires the processor.

Interrupts can be sent by input/output devices such as printers, or by users on a multi-access operating system. Interrupts are also used when operating systems are used in a multi-tasking environment. This can done by a time-slice, i.e. each program is given an allocated slice of time for processor use. When each time-slice is used up, an internal timer sends an interrupt and the next program or activity acquires control of the processor.

Operating Systems

Have you improved?

1 At launch, Microsoft Windows 2000 was termed 'the most comprehensive operating system to date' – it uses a GUI, more specifically the WIMP environment.

a) What is:
   i) a GUI?
   ii) a WIMP environment?

b) Why has the GUI become so popular?

c) List some of the main functions of a modern operating system.

What utilities does your home computer OS provide?

2 Give one example for each of the following types of operating systems.

a) batch

b) real time

c) interactive

d) on-line

3 Operating systems can use interrupts when data is transferred to a printer.

a) Define the role of interrupts in this case.

b) Give another example of the use of interrupts in operating systems.

Networking and Communication

15 mins
Time Yourself

How much do you know?

1 What do LAN and WAN stand for?

2 The theoretical layout of a network is called its __________. The three basic layouts are ____, ____ and ____.

3 List two advantages and two disadvantages of using a network in place of stand-alone machines.

4 Briefly differentiate between serial data communication and parallel data communication.

5 a) Simplex, half duplex and full duplex are all different modes of ______________.

b) The method of data transmission that uses start and stop bits and transfers data as soon as it is available instead of waiting for a clock pulse is known as ______________.

Answers

1 Local Area Network, Wide Area Network **2** topology, star, ring and bus
3 Advantages: sharing of hardware and software resources, i.e. printers and software and the transfer of files from one user to another etc. Disadvantages: complicated systems administration on a network, possible security breaches of confidential information **4** serial data transmission sends one bit at a time, one after the other through a single wire. Parallel data transmission can send more than one bit at a time over more than one wire (i.e. in parallel) **5** transmission, asynchronous

If you got them all right, skip to page 79

Spend no more than 30 mins on this topic

Networking and Communication

Learn the key facts

1 A Local Area Network (LAN) is a network of computers connected together by means of cables or other methods (radio transmission, infrared, blue-tooth, etc), confined to a relatively small area, e.g. a school campus. A Wide Area Network is a network of computers that can be located anywhere as their methods of communicating can handle vast distances (e.g. ISDN, satellites).

2 A network's topology is its theoretical layout. The actual arrangement depends on the location of nodes of the network.

Star networks consist of a central computer to which other computers and devices (nodes) are connected. This form of network can be costly due to the amount of cabling required.

The main advantages of this type of network are:

- If one of the nodes or cables fails, then the other nodes (computers or devices) are not affected.
- The transmission of information from one computer to another is more secure since each machine has its own direct connection to the server.
- Extra nodes (computer, printer etc) can be added without disrupting the network.

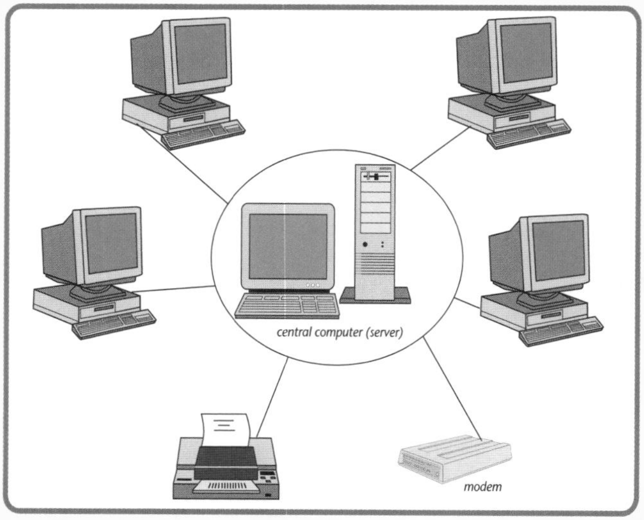

Ring networks consist of a collection of computers connected along a ring (or loop) from which signals are sent (in one direction). The main disadvantage of this type of network is that if one of the nodes fails, then the whole network fails. The main advantage of this kind of network is that it is simple to set up and does not require a server.

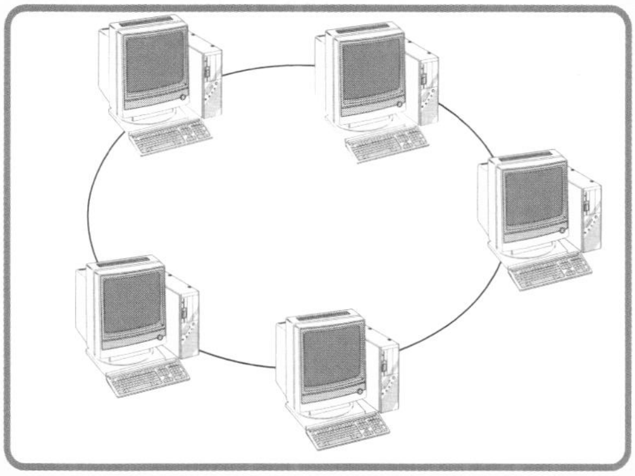

Bus networks consist of a collection of computers and devices all connected along the same single cable. Information can travel in both directions along the cable but only one computer can transmit information at one time. Therefore methods of determining which computer has priority when more than one machine wants to send information are important. The advantages of this type of network are it is simple and cost effective to implement; it is also easy to add extra nodes without disrupting the network.

1
2
3
4
5
DAY 6
7

3 There are several advantages of using a network over stand-alone machines:

- sharing of resources such as hard disk drives, other backing store, printers, scanners, modems;
- sharing of information and files (subject to access rights);
- sharing of software;
- the ability to communicate with other users on the network.

The main disadvantages include the cost of systems administration, disruption caused, and the possibility of security breaches and unauthorised access to confidential and sensitive information.

4 Serial transmission sends data down from source to destination one bit at a time via a single data line. This method of transmission is usually cheaper than parallel transmission as it only requires one line. It is normally used in transferring data over long distances as error correction and control is usually much more practical and cheaper to implement over a single data line. Serial transmissions need not always be slow, as fast transfer rates can be obtained using certain wires or cables such as fibre optics. Parallel transmission allows more than one bit to be transferred from source to destination simultaneously and must therefore use more than one data line. An example of the use of parallel transmission is in printer ports, which can send eight bits simultaneously (in parallel) because they have eight separate data lines.

5 There are three different modes of transmission: simplex, half duplex and full duplex. With the simplex mode of transmission, data can only be sent in one direction, from source to destination. With half duplex, data can be sent in both directions, but only one at a time. Full duplex allows the transmission of data in both directions simultaneously.

For asynchronous transmission, one character is sent at a time, each with a start and stop bit to determine where one character ends and another starts. Often parity bits are included to check if the data has been transmitted correctly. With synchronous transmission, timing signals (usually the computer clock) synchronise the transmission so there is no need for start and stop bits for each character transmitted. They are only required for the complete transmission.

Networking and Communication

30 mins
Time Yourself

Have you improved?

1 A team of solicitors has a number of offices across the country. Each of its offices has a number of stand-alone PCs for the partners and employees. The company wishes to be able to share files across all its PCs, both within the offices and also between offices.

a) Give a reason why a LAN should be used within each of the offices.

b) Give a reason why a WAN should be used between the offices.

c) Suggest, with reasons, a suitable network topology for use within the offices.

computers and networks are designed to make our lives as effortless and disruption-free as possible

2 What information, other than start, stop and parity bits, is required for one computer to communicate with another over a LAN?

how do you know who you are talking to in the dark?

3 Give an example of a network topology for each of the following modes of transmission:

a) simplex

b) half-duplex

c) full duplex.

15 mins

Time Yourself

Systems Development

How much do you know?

1 a) Name five of the different stages of the systems life cycle.

b) Suggest four characteristics of a manual-based system that may make it feasible for computerisation.

c) Give one major objective for implementing a computerised system.

d) List five methods of investigation that could be used to understand the existing manual system and how it could change.

2 What is prototyping?

3 Briefly describe what type of information must be considered when designing a Human Computer Interface (HCI).

4 List at least three different methods of system changeover.

5 Outline why there is a need for systems evaluation and maintenance.

Answers

1 a) problem definition, feasibility study, analysis, design, construction, implementation, maintenance, evaluation b) constant monitoring, need for accuracy, inputting large volume of data, regular batch processing, large amounts of information, data sharing, etc c) increased efficiency of a manual process d) interviewing workers, questionnaires, the observation of work in progress and the inspection of records **2** the method of constructing and running a system to test and evaluate it prior to building the complete system **3** type of people using system, e.g. children; type of task to be performed, e.g. what information is to be displayed; environment in which computer is used, e.g. noise, interference **4** direct changeover, parallel conversion, phased conversion, pilot scheme **5** evaluation is necessary to determine if the system performs its functions well and to detect weaknesses or determine if modifications are required. Maintenance is required if systems need updating due to errors in the system or a change in circumstances

If you got them all right, skip to page 84

Systems Development

Spend no more than 30 mins on this topic

Learn the key facts

1 All commercial computer systems follow a life cycle. Procedures and methods for doing tasks change with time, due to technological change, legislation or other factors. A new system must be implemented and hence the life cycle starts again. The main procedures of the life cycle are demonstrated below.

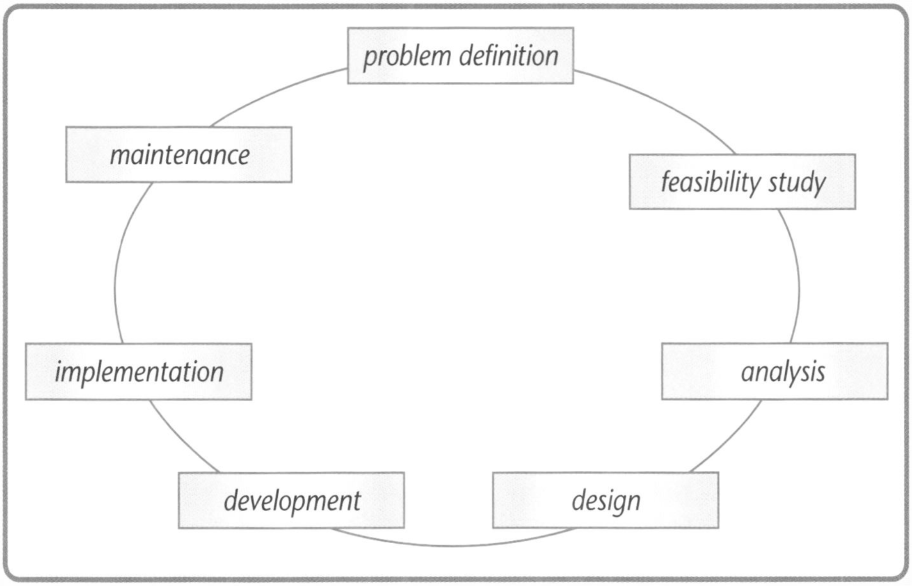

The problem definition outlines the problems or limitations of the current system and the feasibility study examines whether upgrading the system is a feasible option, i.e. the pros and cons. Parts of the feasibility study and analysis may include a report on the current system, objectives for the new system, whether these objectives can be met, a cost-benefit analysis and a timescale for the implementation of the new system. Other methods of carrying out the analysis could include performing interviews, distributing questionnaires and observing current practices. Also, dataflow diagrams and system flowcharts need to be drawn to help understand how the current system works. The design process will consider the input and output of the new system, i.e. the layout (including the user interface), medium and content. Security, processing and types of hardware required are also considered. The program design is then put through various methods of testing – program testing (bottom-up and top-down) and system testing (functional, recovery and performance). The development of the new system involves the coding and testing of programs. This is followed by acceptance testing to determine if the customer feels the system delivers to the original specifications, whether the new system will run in the environment intended and whether any changes need to be made. If the new system fulfils all of the criteria, then the implementation of the system begins. This includes the hardware and software installation, the transfer of necessary files from the old system and possibly the retraining of staff. Documentation for the new system needs to be created, i.e. user manuals, technical manuals and program documentation. Once the system is in place, evaluation and maintenance of the system is carried out.

2 Prototyping is the term given for the construction of the first working model of a computer system in order to evaluate and test the system for approval prior to building the final system. It could involve testing to see if the model responds correctly to commands or the input of data. Users can also experience the design and usability of the system before approval.

3 The user interface is an important aspect of the new system as it is the means for the user to command the system. The design of the user interface must take into consideration who may use the system and what they will use the system for. Also, aspects such as the environment in which the unit is to be used must be taken into consideration.

4 Implementation of the new system is an important aspect of the process. The main methods of proceeding with the changeover include direct changeover, which involves the complete removal of the old system and the installation of the new, usually over a weekend or during a less busy period. This method is risky because of the possibility of the new system failing but is sometimes unavoidable if the new system is completely different from the old, or if restrictions such as time and storage space apply. Parallel conversion usually involves the continuing use of the old system alongside the new for a short amount of time so that the progress of the new system can be checked against that of the old. The advantage of this is that if the new system does fail, the old system can still be continued. However, the disadvantage is the effort required to run both systems. Phased conversion usually means the implementation of the new system in phases, i.e. breaking the system into parts and introducing the new system one part at a time. Pilot conversion methods usually involve a new system being introduced into one branch or department and then, if it works well, being extended to other branches and departments.

5 Evaluation and maintenance are important in the period after the system is up and running to ensure that the new system runs according to expectations. If there are any small modifications necessary for whatever reason, these can then be carried out. Maintenance allows the system to run smoothly and provides ongoing bug fixes. The system can be updated if any changes to circumstances arise. Maintenance can be classified into three types: perfective maintenance, which is the process of making improvements (i.e. trying to perfect the system), adaptive maintenance, which is the process of adapting the system to changes in requirements or legislation, and corrective maintenance, which is correcting any errors that arise.

30 mins

Time Yourself

Systems Development

Have you improved?

1 a) Why is it important to test a computerised system fully before it is installed?

b) Name two methods of program testing.

c) Name three types of system testing.

2 Other than the costs of the hardware and software, list at least three other costs of systems development that must be considered .

3 Many people fear the introduction of computers into the work place. Discuss this issue and suggest methods of alleviating this concern

are any members of your family computer-phobic?

Exam Practice Questions

60 mins
Time Yourself

1 Validation checks can be used to prevent errors in data being input into a computer system. Give three examples of validation checks and for each give an example of invalid data that could be detected by it. (3 marks)

2 Personal computers have a variety of disk drives available. Describe the purposes and approximate capacities of (a) hard disk drives (b) floppy disk drives and (c) CD-ROM drives. (6 marks)

3 Data can be transmitted across networks by a variety of protocols. Also, simplex, full duplex or half duplex methods may be used. Explain what is meant by:
a) protocols
b) simplex
c) full duplex
d) half duplex. (8 marks)

4 A high level programming language supports integer, real (floating point), string and boolean data types. Using examples, explain the meaning of these different data types and for each, comment on the amount of memory storage required. (8 marks)

5 Explain the meaning of a multi-tasking operating system. Explain how interrupts can be used in order to allow multi-tasking. (4 marks)

6 a) Explain the meaning of the term 'bus' in computer hardware. (1 mark)
b) Describe the purpose of two buses that connect the processor to main memory. (2 marks)

7 A music shop keeps details of CDs on computer file. The information that is stored includes the CD's reference number, the performers, the label and how many are in stock. These details are kept in an indexed sequential file.
a) Explain and justify a choice of key field for this file. (2 marks)
b) Describe how the index can be used to search for details of a particular CD. (2 marks)
c) Describe an alternative fast method of file access and explain how it is used to find a particular record in the file. (3 marks)

8 A software developer writes a program for a client using a high level language. He develops the program using an interpreter. When he has finished, he compiles the source code to object code.

a) Explain the difference between an interpreter and a compiler. (2 marks)

b) Explain one advantage of using an interpreter at the development stage. (2 marks)

c) Describe the difference between source code and object code. (2 marks)

d) Give two reasons why the developer would not normally give his or her client the source code. (2 marks)

9 a) Describe what is meant by the term 'batch processing'. (2 marks)

b) Give one situation where batch processing is suitable and explain why this is so. (3 marks)

10 When a new system is developed, testing, implementation and maintenance stages form part of the process.

a) Describe two methods of testing software. (4 marks)

b) State two events that occur during the implementation stage. (2 marks)

c) Give two circumstances that make maintenance necessary. (2 marks)

(total 60 marks)

Hints

Generally, try to judge how many points to make in each answer by looking at the mark allocation.

Recognise the difference between questions that say 'state' and those that say 'describe' or 'explain'. 'State' requires a simple fact. 'Describe' or 'explain' questions will normally have an additional mark allocation for an expansion on the basic fact.

If the answer to a question seems obvious, it is probably right. Don't go looking for hidden meaning. Examiners are not trying to trick you, they simply want to give you a chance to show what you know and what you can do.

Make an attempt at all the required questions. Remember, a blank response guarantees zero! A hunch just may be right.

Check that you have attempted all the questions you are supposed to. There have been many cases where candidates have overlooked the back page of the question sheet.

Answers on page 95

Have you improved: Answers

An Introduction to Computers

1 a) Stock control and order processing usually require the computer to log all purchases made and thus monitor the amount of stock for each item. This is usually done by means of a barcode reader. Each time an item is scanned in from the barcode reader for a sale, the stock number for that item is reduced. Once the stock level reaches a certain point the computer processes an order to replenish the stock.

b) Computers control the timing and order of traffic lights systems, e.g. during rush hour the lights may change more regularly or give more time to a certain side of a junction. Also there could be traffic sensors in some lanes, which give traffic in that lane priority (e.g. buses). The computer systems read these sensors and adjust the traffic signals accordingly, usually to a set program.

2 If the current boom in Internet banks continues and fewer people use the traditional high street banks, this could mean the closure of many of these high street branches as there is less cost involved in Internet transactions and there may not be enough demand to keep high street branches open.

3 The initial cost of robots could be expensive. Robots may not properly detect visual manufacturing flaws. Unskilled workers may lose their jobs.

4 Embedded computers have made the operation of household goods such as televisions, washing machines and microwaves extremely user-friendly. Offering simple pre-programmed instructions for use, e.g. washing programmes, means that we just select a program for the type of wash we want and leave the washing machine to do the rest. Some microwaves allow the user to select the food they are cooking and the microwave will cook the food without further input.

People and Computers

1 Cost of hardware and software installation; maintenance costs; redundancy costs of laying off unskilled workers; costs of retraining employees and hiring new staff.

2 In case of systems failures or unauthorised changes to current data/information on the system; keeping old customers' details for future reference; auditing, etc.

3 The development of software is often a lengthy and difficult process. Many man-hours are used writing and developing programs for commercial gain. The unauthorised copying of copyrighted materials often undermines all the hard work that programmers and developers have gone through. This can often cause financial and other hardship for the individuals and companies that produce this software, forcing them out of business. All too often this causes the prices of other software to rise and deters many potential software writers from entering the market and producing quality work.

4 Many believe that the monitoring of others is a breach of privacy rights. Although there are unscrupulous people who misuse computers, the majority of computer users do not. Many innocent people feel uneasy at the thought that their private actions are being monitored. Data and information stored about people and their actions can often be misinterpreted. If the information is stored, this could be in breach of the Data Protection Act.

5 a) There are many different uses of sophisticated filters. The use of these filters in search engines allows users to find details or information quickly and easily as the filters only show the most likely matches to a search.

b) Sophisticated filters can be used over the Internet to prohibit access to restricted sites or anti-social materials.

6 Most computerised systems in industry are designed to replace manual systems. They provide easier and more efficient methods or means of performing a task.

a) Given that many computerised systems can be set to perform a variety of different tasks, the end user must be able to operate the machine properly if the machine is to be effective. Therefore user support is essential.

b) If a technical difficulty or problem arises, it is often important to rectify the problem as soon as possible. This aid comes in the form of technical support.

Software

1 a) Spreadsheets do not usually have the ability to produce complex structural links between the data held on file.

b) Database.

c) Software with a variety of different applications to perform different functions, but usually with integrated features to allow portability between the individual application functions. Integrated packages usually include a word processor, spreadsheet, database, etc.

d) The integrated function may not perform the required tasks. There may not be a need for all of the functions of an integrated package and it would be more cost-effective just to purchase an individual application.

e) Bespoke software is usually much more expensive than commercial software. Commercial software is also easier to obtain and install (i.e. purchase off-the-shelf and install). Testing for bugs is usually much more thorough as many people will have bought the package beforehand. The bespoke software may be custom-made to provide all the facilities required, which the commercial package may not provide.

2 a) Microsoft Word, Lotus AmiPro, WordPerfect, etc.

b) Microsoft Excel, Lotus 1-2-3, SuperCalc.

c) Microsoft Access, Paradox, FoxPro.

Hardware

1 As the performance of microcomputers gets more powerful with new multiprocessor systems, and storage capacity increases whilst accommodating much less physical space, microcomputers are increasingly more capable of being used in place of basic mainframe computers. The price difference between micro and mainframe computers is still substantial, yet many of the mainframe functions can be substituted with basic workstations connected to powerful microcomputers, there may soon be a considerable overlap of use between powerful microcomputer and mainframe machines. This is likely to be contributed to by the compatibility of today's microcomputers as opposed to specialist computers usually associated with mainframe systems.

2 The three standard buses are the data bus (two way) – needed to carry the data to and from the CPU and memory; the address bus (one way) – needed to carry the location of memory address; and the control bus (two way) – needed to carry the signal to tell the memory whether a read or write is in operation.

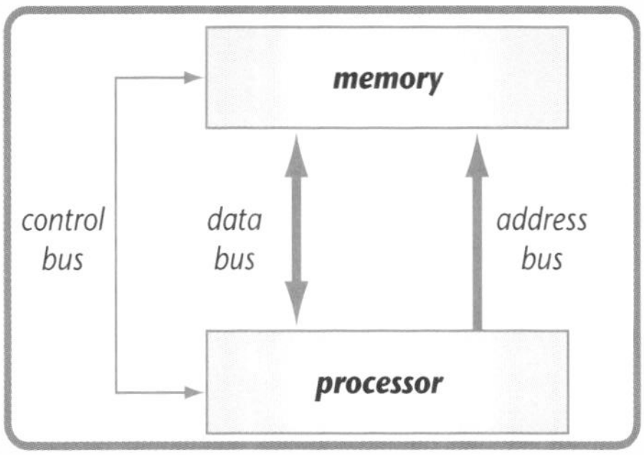

3 a) CD-ROMs, CD-Rs and CD-RWs as a backing store are more durable than conventional tapes. They are harder, and less prone to damage from handling and dust than tapes. Searching and retrieving data from a CD is usually much faster than from tapes. CDs offer a much more compatible form of distributing data as most people with computers have a CD-ROM drive but may not necessarily have a compatible tape drive.

b) Many people do not need or want to change their existing system, as they only archive or backup data for their own reference and their existing system is suitable for their needs. Thus, upgrading their backup system from tape to CD is an unnecessary expenditure.

Data Storage

1 a) A series of contour measurements.

b) A series of frequencies or note values.

c) A series of test scores.

2 a) OMR, smart card.

b) (i) and (ii)

3 a) (i) 31 (ii) −1 (iii) −127 (iv) −29

b) (i) 1F (ii) 11 (iii) FF (iv) 41

4 $512 \times 256 = 131072$ bytes (each byte can code for 256 colours because it consists of 8 bits).

5

Surname:	string	say 15 bytes
Forename:	string	say 15 bytes
No. of books on loan:	integer	2 bytes
Fine due:	Boolean	1 byte
Total storage:		33 bytes (adjust as necessary for reasonable string sizes)

Data Structures

1 a) A one dimensional array of string type.

b) The element containing the string 'July' would be referenced by its index, in this case 7, e.g.

```
month_name = months(7)
```

2 a) A queue. As it is a FIFO structure, the aircraft would be landed in the order in which they arrived.

b) An array of records. Each record would be structured to hold the required details. Two integers would also be required to hold the positions of the front and the back of the queue.

Have you improved: Answers

3 a) Array holds the data items to go in the stack. Integer is top of stack pointer.
b) Array is static – memory wasted on unused stack positions; also restricts flexibility in stack size.

4 Binary tree. Each word is a node and contains pointers to words before and after. Suitable because the word being searched for requires relatively few comparisons to be made before finding correct word.

5 The item immediately before the required deletion has the pointer adjusted to point to the item immediately after the deleted item.

Files

1 Binary file.

2 a) ISBN.

b) For each record, assume: 13 bytes for ISBN; 20 bytes for author; 5 bytes for publisher code; 6 bytes for a floating point number; 2 bytes for category.
Total = 46 per record. Multiply by 10 000 (titles) = 460000. Add on, say, 512 bytes for overheads = 460512. Equivalent to about 450 Kbytes.

3 Serial number should not exceed a maximum length; date purchased must be within reasonable limits such as not in the future; category should not exceed expected length.

4 Variable-length fields waste less space than fixed-length fields, so transmission times will be reduced.

5

456	Sector 56
876	Sector 76
645	Sector 45
856	Sector 56
956	Overflow

Data Security and Integrity

1 A virus is a malicious program designed to be copied onto many computers and files. Hacking is the illegal accessing of private data.

2 Two of: virus scanning software; update scanning software; quarantine suspect machines; prevent use of disks brought in from outside; block suspect web sites.

3 a) Backing up only new and updated files.
b) Between full backups, to save time.

Have you improved: Answers

4 a) All sales totals are added up from source data. This sum is regenerated from the transaction file data. The two sums are compared. Any discrepancy is highlighted.

b) A sum is calculated based on all the stock numbers of all the sales. This is compared with the transaction file data. Any discrepancy indicates an error and is highlighted.

Programming (1)

1 A low level language is machine oriented; each instruction achieves just one machine operation. A high level language is problem oriented; each statement results in many machine operations.

2 Part of memory is reserved to hold a value that will be referred to by name by the programmer. Type checking is also enabled, which helps to prevent some programming errors.

3 a) 9

b) 7.5

c) 4

d) 22

4 A variety of answers are possible and the language used will vary slightly in syntax, but in Visual BASIC an approach could be:

```
Dim count As Integer
Dim total As Double
total = 0
For count = 1 To 5
total = total + InputBox("Enter a number")
Next
Call av(total, count - 1)
End Sub
Sub av(num_1 As Double, num_2 As Integer)
Dim result As Double
result = num_1 / num_2
MsgBox (result)
End Sub
```

The number of iterations may be fixed and known in advance (for…next), they may need to be tested on entry to (do….while) or exit from (repeat until) the loop.

Have you improved: Answers

Programming (2)

1 There is no need for translation at run time; the processor runs object code.

2
```
input sides
for count = 1 to sides
line
left 360 / sides
next
```

3 It is easier to concentrate on small modules and easier to co-ordinate the work of many programmers if they are all working to the same specifications.

4 Any syntax error such as a mis-spelt key word or a faulty construct such as 'repeat' without 'until'.

5 Test data is designed to expose any errors in the logic of a program. It should be chosen to cover normal, extreme and erroneous cases.

Operating Systems

1 a) (i) GUI (Graphical User Interface). A method of communication between people and computers with the use of graphical displays, i.e. boxes, pictures, icons.
(ii) WIMP (Windows Icons Menus Pointer) environment. A GUI uses a mouse (or other device), which moves a visual cursor to launch and control applications by clicking on icons and menus.

b) GUIs have become extremely popular because they are easier to learn and use than traditional command-based interfaces.

c) Memory management, input and output, resource allocation, interrupt handling, file management, security, etc.

2 a) The production of monthly utility bills.

b) Air traffic control systems.

c) Cash machines.

d) Cash machines.

3 a) When data is to be transferred to the printer an interrupt is generated and sent to suspend the current running program. The data to be printed is processed and sent to the printer. Once the processor has finished with the printing process, the initial program resumes.

b) Interrupts can be generated once a time-slice has expired.

Have you improved: Answers

Networking and Communication

1 a) No cost for sending data across the LAN; ease of distributing files between staff; the sharing of resources in the offices, etc.

b) WAN is the only practical method of connecting computers via a network over a wide geographical area. Files and cases can be sent to one office for archiving and backup, etc.

c) Star topology. The transmission of information between computers is more secure as each computer has its own direct connection to the server. If a cable or computer connected to the network fails, it does not disrupt the other computers in the network. Computers and other devices can be connected without disrupting the network.

2 The identification of the source and destination computers is required so that the data arrives at the correct terminal.

3 a) ring

b) bus

c) star

Systems Development

1 a) A computerised system must be fully tested to ensure that all of its parts perform the functions that they were designed for, as well as to ensure that the system is bug-free.

b) Bottom-up testing and top-down testing.

c) Functional testing – ensuring the system functions correctly. Recovery testing – ensuring the system can recover from various forms of failure. Performance testing – testing the performance of the system under various conditions

2 Installation costs, retraining costs, redundancy costs, extra security costs, etc.

3 Many people are afraid that they may not be able to use the new technology and that they may lose their jobs or position of power as a result. There are various methods of trying to alleviate this problem, such as offering training before the system is installed, and counselling and advice during operation.

Exam Practice: Answers

The following are possible answers. In many cases, the examiner's mark scheme will allow other correct responses.

1 Type check: e.g. a number entered into a text field such as a person's surname.
Range check: e.g. an applicant for a job with a date of birth obviously too long ago or too recent.
Check digit: e.g. a mistyped digit in a bank account number.

Note that the question requires the checks to be identified plus an example. Both parts are required for the mark.

2 a) Hard disk drive: storage of user's programs and data, capacity between 1 and 30 gigabytes.
b) Floppy disk drives: backup, transfer of data from one computer to another, capacity 1.44 megabytes.
c) CD-ROMs, software distribution, archiving data, multimedia; capacity 600 megabytes–1 gigabyte.

Make sure you can quote reasonable figures for hardware configurations.

3 a) Rules which control the format of messages sent between devices so that they can understand each other.
b) Transmission of signals in one direction only.
c) Transmission of signals in both directions at the same time.
d) Transmission of signals in both directions but not at the same time.

4 Integer: whole numbers, usually 1, 2 or 4 bytes.
Real: numbers with fractional part (can be very large or very small), 6 to 12 bytes.
String: collection of characters, up to 255 bytes.
Boolean: yes/no data, 1 byte maximum.

5 Multi-tasking means the ability seemingly to run more than one program at a time. An interrupt is a signal that stops the execution of current task and diverts the processor's attention to another task. The processor later resumes the original task. Rapid switching between tasks gives the impression of simultaneous execution.

6 a) A bus is a set of wires which carries signals between components in a computer system.
b) The address bus carries the address of the memory location to be accessed. The data bus carries the contents of a specified memory location. The control buses carry signals such as to start and stop a process or indicate an error condition.

Exam Practice: Answers

7 a) The key field will be reference number. This is because it uniquely identifies a record.

b) The index is searched to find the block which contains the record required. Then the block is searched.

c) An alternative method is to calculate the address of the record using a hashing algorithm. The key field is transformed to produce this address.

Remember that most data tables will have key fields. These are often reference numbers of some sort, but may sometimes be combined fields.

8 a) Interpreter translates and executes source code line by line. Compiler translates source code but does not execute it.

b) Lines of code can be tried out in isolation.

c) Source code is the high level program as written. It cannot be executed by the processor. Object code is the translated program which can be executed directly.

d) The source code requires the customer to have translation software; object code is less likely to be altered by the user.

9 a) Data is gathered together, then processed in one go.

b) A payroll is a suitable case, as the hours worked and other data are gathered together and all the records have to be processed.

10 a) Dry run: program flow is checked outside the computer system, or debugging software is used to examine variables or registers as the program executes. Alternatively, black box testing: inputs are checked so that they give the correct outputs. White box testing is used to examine all the paths through the software with the input of normal, extreme or bad data.

b) The\intenance is necessary when there are still bugs to be sorted out, requirements have changed or new features are required.